# Johnny Lazarus in MOUNTAIN MIRACLE!

## Written and Illustrated by
# Keith Poletiek

*OLIVIA—*
*GOD BLESS!*
*Keith Poletiek*

316 STUDIOS PUBLICATION
©Copyright 2017 Wide Open Productions

# A MOUNTAIN OF THANKS!

Let's Start at the Top!
Thank you to my God above
and my Lord, Jesus Christ
for your love and allowing me
to share You through
these adventures.

Thank you to my family
who tolerates a storyteller
who has a hard time
shutting down.

Thank you to the
WideOpen Production
(Now 316Studios) Team
for bringing Johnny to Life!

Thank you Vicky Stevens
for the many hours spent trying
to make my scribbles readable.

Thank you, as always, to
all my family and friends
who have supported me
over the years.

You All Rock!

# CONTENTS

# A NOTE FROM
## The Author

Once again, I take on the role of Johnny (a much cooler name than Keith) in this fourth Johnny Lazarus book, "Mountain Miracle!" It's another crazy adventure based partly on a past experience that changed my life forever. Hopefully, it will give you some great insight about trusting God even when you don't think you can. I also hope you will continue to have a great love for God's creation even though I struggled, at the time, to enjoy the mountaintop experience my dad had taken my brother Steve and me on back when we were young.

At one point, I never wanted to hear the phrase, "God's Great Outdoors," again, let alone go up a mountain, or hill, or over a speed bump! I figured this one trip, high in the mountains, and everything that happened to me there, was enough for a lifetime.

"Do you want to go hiking, Keith?"

"No, I'm good."

"Do you want to sign up for camp?"

"In the mountains? No, I'm still good!"

"Do you want to jump off the curb?"

"Too high. I'm good!"

Fear can be hard to conquer, but I found a secret to making it easier…"trust." Trust is an amazing thing. Learning to trust myself and others a bit more got me through some scary times. Putting my trust in God, however, well, that was the BIG game changer, especially in *this* backpacking adventure. Only trusting God could help me out of this mountain of trouble! Enjoy!

Keith (Johnny Lazarus) Poletiek

# CHAPTER ONE
## "WHAT'S BACKPACKING?"

"What in the world are these?" I said to myself, spotting the three crazy-big objects sitting in the middle of the living room floor when I walked in the house from school.

At twelve years old, I thought I had pretty much seen everything, but nothing like these before. I mean, I knew they were backpacks. Duh! But they weren't like the ones I, or any kid, wore to school. These were backpacks on steroids! They were at least three feet tall and two feet wide, and I began thinking, "If my mom and dad try to make me wear one of these bad boys to school, I'm never going back!"

They were not only big, but bright colors as well, and I guessed could probably carry a thousand pounds of books, easy.

"What are these things?" I shouted, though there was no one in the room.

"They're backpacks, Johnny," my dad said, as he walked in from the kitchen.

"I'm not wearing one of these to school!" I said in a panic. My dad just laughed and so did my older brother, Steve, as he walked in the room, followed by my mom.

"They're for backpacking in the mountains, genius," my brother said sarcastically.

"The mountains" I questioned? "We're going backpacking in the mountains? Cool! Which one is mine?"

"Mine is the blue one," my brother, Steve, said.
"Dad's is the orange one and yours is the green one because green is for dorks."

"Ha. Ha. Very funny," I fired back.

It was such a big brother's response. Steve and I were good friends, but like most brothers, also rivals at times. And, of course, there were times he could make me so mad I didn't want to be around him at all! Yet, I knew if I was ever in real trouble, he was the first person I wanted by my side, and he would usually come running when I needed him. So, I put up with the occasional *dork* comment or whatever he came up with to call me.

Actually, I was lucky. He was a pretty good big brother as big brothers go. I learned a lot from him. He was great at just about any sport and taught me how to shoot my first jump shot, throw my first curveball and land my first Ollie on a skateboard. Besides, we each had our own rooms, so if he ever bothered me too much, I could always escape to mine and be done with him for awhile.

"Uh-oh! I'm going to be trapped in the mountains with him for days! What if he gets on my nerves then?" I wondered.

There's no place to run to and nowhere to hide out there, unless I wanted to run off into the forest and never be heard from again! Maybe this backpacking-thing wasn't so *cool* after all.

"How long are we going backpacking for, dad?" I wanted to know how long I had to tolerate Steve before I might have to become a mountain dweller for the rest of my life.

"Three days and two nights," my dad said. "It will be just the three of us alone with nature, high in the mountains and living off the land."

"Living off the land?" I said nervously. "We're not going to have to hunt for our food, are we?"

"That's what the backpacks are for, dweeb!" My brother said sharply. "They carry all the food we'll need, right, dad?"

"Most of it," dad said. "Though, we might try our hand at a little fishing. I hear the mountain trout taste pretty good cooked over an open flame!"

My dad picked up one of the packs and showed us everything about it. He showed us where to adjust and tighten the straps so the pack would fit just right on our shoulders. Then he went over each pouch and pocket on all sides and what could go in them.

"All the clothes you'll need goes in here along with your portion of the food to carry and any supplies you might need. We'll roll up and tie your sleeping bag and mat to the bottom, and your First Aid Kit goes in here."

He went on for another five minutes telling us what we would be carrying and I started to think I'd never be able to carry all that on my back, not to mention wearing it while walking up a mountain.

"This won't be an easy trip," my dad said. "But it will be rewarding and you'll get to see a part of God's creation that few people ever get to see. You'll remember this adventure forever."

"If I live through it," I thought.

"What about bears and snakes and scorpions?" I asked.

"Yep," was all that my dad said.

"Yep? What kind of answer was that?" I thought. "Yep, they'll be there, but they won't bother us, or 'Yep,' they'll be there and our lives will be in constant danger?"

"We'll be fine," my dad said with confidence. "We'll leave

them alone and they'll leave us alone. We'll tie our food up high in the trees to keep the bears from getting at it and we'll keep a fire going at night to keep most of the critters away."

"Most of the critters?" I questioned. "I'm starting to not like the sound of this backpacking-thing after all. What if we just go into the mountains and stay in a cabin or nice lodge instead. I'll sleep on the floor, and we can call that roughing it!"

"Relax, Johnny, this is going to be a blast," my brother Steve said. "Dad wouldn't put our lives in jeopardy. Well, at least, not mine anyway. I'm his favorite son. You, however, are expendable. We might have to feed you to a bear of it comes to that."

"Ha! Ha! Very funny," I said…but it wasn't.

"Do you really think we can do this, dad?" I asked. "We've never been backpacking before."

"It won't be the easiest thing you've ever done, but it might just be one of the most rewarding," he said. "Hiking into the wilderness, seeing the trees, the rocks, the rivers and nature in all its splendor will be well worth it. And, the view of the valley from ten thousand feet will give you memories that will last a lifetime."

"Wait! Did you just say ten thousand feet?" I said with that panicked voice, again. "We're going to hike to ten thousand feet?"

"I'll have memories that will last a lifetime all right! Because if I try to climb to ten thousand feet I'll be dead in a day!"

"Calm down, sissy-brain!" My brother shouted.

Sissy-brain? That was a new one!

"You guys will do fine," my dad said, once again with confidence. "As long as you practice enough before we leave - which is in less than a week. We hit the trail this Saturday, so you need to put in some time practicing backpacking."

"Practicing backpacking?" I thought to myself. "How do I

practice backpacking? Do I go climb the nearest mountain a few times until I pass out? Do I head to the zoo and wrestle a couple of bears? How does someone practice backpacking?"

Climbing the nearest mountain wouldn't work anyway because there weren't any mountains around here for miles. There were some dirt hills out behind our housing tract but that's where the cool bike riders would hang out and practice awesome bike maneuvers. I wouldn't want to be seen walking around with this big, bright green monster on my back. They would laugh me back to third grade for sure!

Maybe, I could watch something about backpacking techniques on YouTube. Someone must have done a video about how to put a large pack on your back and walk straight up forever. Or, maybe I should head down to our local bookstore and see if they have the book, "Backpacking For Dummies!"

Or, maybe I should just ask my dad.

But, before I could ask, my dad explained what to do. He told us we should go in our rooms and fill our backpacks with stuff to make them heavy and then put them on and spend some time walking around the neighborhood. This would get us use to walking with weight on our shoulders and strengthen our legs for the three day journey. That made sense to me, so I grabbed my *dorky-green* backpack and headed to my room to fill it up. If I was going to do this backpacking-thing I was going to be prepared. Maybe, if I practiced really hard I'd even be better at backpacking than my older brother, Steve.

"Fat chance!" I thought.

Like I said before, my brother was great at everything. Why would backpacking be any different? And, do you think he'd let me be? No way!

When I got to my room I looked around to see what I should put in my backpack to fill it up. I began to wonder what my brother Steve was putting in his backpack. Maybe I should take a quick peek and see. I'm going to need every advantage I can find if I'm going to make it through this ten thousand foot high journey and live to tell about it.

Chapter 1 Word Study & Doodle on Pages 114-115

# CHAPTER TWO
## "PRACTICE MAKES PERFECT!"

Of course, when I went to see what my brother was putting into his backpack his door was shut and locked. Looks like I'll have to figure things out for myself, so I headed to my room. I leaned my backpack against my bed so it would stay standing and opened the big flap on the top.

"What to put in first?" I thought.

I started with clothes, pants first. I pulled out three pair of pants, one pair for each day. I never knew how heavy pants really were, though, until I was holding the three pairs in my arms. They seemed way too heavy to carry for three days, and they were only the first item.

"I can wear the same pair for all three days," I decided. So, I just put one pair of pants in.

I did the same with my shirts - one shirt. I then went with one pair of underwear, and one sock. "No, I might need two – socks. Yeah, two socks."

I figured I could sleep on the ground near the fire at night and use a rock for a pillow so I didn't attach any bedding to the bottom of the pack where dad had told us it would go. I would make sure I didn't get hurt on the trip, so no First Aid Kit, and if I just ate the trout I caught I wouldn't need to pack any food.

I lifted my pack with its one pair of pants, one shirt, one pair of undies and two socks and thought to myself, "This back-packing-thing is going to be easy."

I threw the backpack over my shoulders, adjusted the straps, snapped the buckle on the belt around my waist and headed for the great outdoors - my cul-de-sac.

My brother was still in his room with his door shut. He, too, was filling his backpack.

"At least I was faster than him at something," I thought.

When I got to the front of the house my mom and dad weren't around, so I decided to head out into the neighborhood on my own.

I made it across the porch, down the driveway and onto the sidewalk in front of my house with ease. I started gaining confidence about backpacking in the mountains with every step I took, but, I had only gone downhill to that point. I hadn't done any uphill climbing yet. So, I walked back up the driveway and to my porch again to see if I could handle the steep foot or two incline.

"No problem," I thought. "Bring on the mountain!"
I walked the sidewalk around our street and then headed over to the street next to mine. I figured I'd walk to the school a few streets over in our housing tract like I did every morning.

"How far is that?" I thought. I wasn't great at distances but I figured it had to be a good ten miles because it took me a good ten minutes to walk there every morning.
I finished two streets and wasn't feeling the massive weight of the backpack and all its contents slowing me down. I passed a few neighbors as I walked and gave them a wave, but I hadn't seen any of my friends until I got to the school.

A bunch of guys had a serious basketball game going on,

my favorite sport. I loved when all the good players got together like this and played because good competition makes for good basketball. I wanted to take my backpack off right then and jump in the game, but I didn't. If I was going to add backpacking to my list of accomplishments, just like basketball, I needed to put in the practice.

When Coastal Eddie, my good friend, saw me walking up with a giant, bright green backpack on my back he stopped dribbling and just stared at me. Pretty soon the entire game stopped and everyone was staring at me in amazement. My best friends, Henry and Richie, were also in the game and came running over to me.

"How much homework do you have?" Henry said, staring at the backpack.

"That's not a backpack for homework you goofball," Richie said to him. "That's a backpack for backpacking like in the jungle or the mountains. Are you going on an African Safari, Johnny? Can I come? I've wanted to write a paper on the different tribes in the South African Plains and this would give me first-hand knowledge!"

Was Richie kidding? What twelve-year-old kid has been longing to write a paper on South African anything?

"Only, Richie, of course," I thought to myself.

If there was anyone our age interested in stuff like that it was Richie. It was also why he was the only one besides me who knew what I had on my back, and I had to be told by my dad. Richie was much smarter than Henry and I, and all the guys on the court combined.

"But, we aren't close to the jungle or the mountains, Johnny, so what gives?" Richie asked.

"My dad, my brother and I are going backpacking for three days in the mountains this weekend," I said. "It will be just the three of us, alone, in the wilderness."

"Nice knowing you," Henry quipped. "Every time the news talks about people that go walking into the wilderness it's because they end up missing. They find them days later either dead because of starvation or they're eaten by mountain lions – or both! Hey, maybe you could take Richie with you. That way I could have both of your bikes and skateboards when you're gone for good."

"What a great friend, Henry," Richie said sarcastically. "Please think happy thoughts of us while we're being mauled by bears, or something."

"No one is getting mauled or eaten, guys," I said with a laugh.

"You don't know for sure, Johnny." Henry replied. "When it all goes bad, it's survival of the fittest out there and I know your brother, Steve! He wouldn't think twice about chomping on your leg if he thought it would keep him alive another day!"

"Nobody is going to be chomping anyone's leg, Henry," Richie said with disgust. "Johnny's dad will be there and see to that."

"I don't know about that," Henry fired back. "I've seen him do some serious damage to a plate of ribs at a church picnic!"

"Be quiet, already!" I shouted at Henry. "I need to go practice backpacking some more. My dad said it won't be easy climbing in the mountains for three days with this pack on my back, so I need to put some miles in before we go."

"Why don't you take a break from practicing backpacking and get in this game for awhile," Coastal Eddie shouted from the court. "We could use another good player in here. These Bozos don't know what they're doing! You could probably take them with your backpack on!"

Wow, a compliment and an invitation to play ball from Coastal Eddie, the coolest kid in the school. This was huge! I didn't dare turn him down. No one turned Coastal Eddie down on anything! But, in a few days I was going to be thrust into the mountains and expected to hike to ten thousand feet and do it without crying in front of my brother, my dad or any wild animals!

"Never let them see your fear," I've always been told. "If they sense fear – they pounce!" That went for the animals *and* my brother - so, backpacking practice would definitely have to come first.

"Maybe next time, Eddie (if there would ever be a next time now that I was turning him down)," I said. "But, I need to put in the time if I'm going to get this backpacking thing down."

Coastal Eddie should understand what kind of effort it takes to be good at stuff. Eddie was great at everything. Even better than my brother at most things, so he will respect me for my decision, right?

"Loser!" Eddie shouted.

Or, maybe he won't.

"Let's go, guys," Eddie said to Henry and Richie.

I'm pretty sure they wanted to talk with me more about my upcoming backpacking adventure, but this was Coastal Eddie calling them. So, they looked at me, shrugged their shoulders and ran back towards the court. Henry put his hand up to his ear like he was holding a phone and mouthed, "Call me later," silently as he ran.

I gave him a quick thumbs-up, turned and stared at the fence at the far end of the school field and started walking.

It would normally take me about two to three minutes to walk to that fence, so I figured it must be about two or three miles away, right?

"This backpacking-thing is going to be a piece of cake!" I said to myself. "Ooh, cake! That sounds awesome! I'm sure I'll have room for few slices of cake in my backpack!"

Chapter 2 Word Study & Doodle on Pages 116-117

# CHAPTER THREE
## "MOUNTAIN MEMORIES"

Every day, after school, I would finish my homework, sometimes, and then throw my backpack on and head out to do a little more "backpacking practice." I needed to put in as many miles as possible if I was going to be ready for our backpacking excursion this coming weekend. Besides, I still wanted to impress my dad with my mad backpacking skills, and do my best to finally be as good, or better, than my brother at something. My brother hadn't practiced all week. In fact, his backpack just sat in the corner of his room, untouched. Didn't he know how hard it would be to hike to ten thousand feet in the mountains? I know he was good at almost everything, but backpacking just might be bit more of a challenge than basketball, baseball, surfing, swimming, skateboarding, soccer, bike riding and everything else he was awesome at doing.

"Fat chance again!" I thought. Steve would throw his backpack on (for the first time) at the bottom of the mountain and sprint to the top. We'd arrive hours later, exhausted, and find he had a fire going and three freshly caught trout cooking in a skillet. A heavy cast iron skillet he had decided to carry in his pack just for sport! I was going to lose this backpacking challenge, big time.

As I returned from another exhausting thirty-minute trek around the neighborhood, I saw Summer Breeze, my next door neighbor and good friend, sitting on her front lawn. I hadn't really seen her all week because of my highly intensive backpacking workouts. When she saw me walking up the street with a giant backpack on my back she laughed at the sight.

"Are you running away from home, Johnny?" She asked, jokingly. "Life can't be that bad, can it? Do you need me to talk you through your troubles?"

"Ha! Ha!" I said back, sarcastically. If this had been Henry or Richie teasing me like this I would have given them an earful, and then taken off the backpack and beaned them in the head with it. But, this was Summer Breeze, and for some reason, she could get away with saying just about anything to me and it would be okay. I always got that funny feeling around her like I wanted her to be my best friend but guys and girls my age don't become best friends, do they? Henry and Richie called it love and never missed a chance to tease me about how much time I spent with her.

Most of our time we spent together was just talking. She was a good talker and an even better listener. She was cute, too. I could talk to her, listen to her and look at her for hours. At least until Henry or Richie would come on the scene. Then I'd be up and ready to leave before the onslaught of jokes began.

"Have you and your wife decided what you're having for dinner?" Henry might say if he caught us together.

"Looks more like they are trying to decide what color curtains to have in their house when they get married," Richie would chime in. Then they would both just laugh and laugh.

I secretly believed they were both jealous because they didn't have someone like Summer in their lives. So, I let them have their fun, but not too much fun - and even when I took off my pack and sat down next to Summer I glanced around to make sure neither of them were in the area.

"My dad is taking me and my brother backpacking in the mountains this weekend," I told her. "So, I need to get in as much backpacking practice as possible before we go."

"How long will you be gone?" Summer asked.

"We are going to be gone for three days. We will be living off the land and sleeping outdoors and everything," I said with excitement.

"Alone in the mountains? Are you scared?" She asked.

Now, to Henry and Richie, or anyone else, I probably would have said, "No way! I'm good!" But this was Summer Breeze asking. Summer was different. I could never fool her, and for some reason, I never really wanted to. She always brought out the honesty in me – most of the time. Besides, Summer could always tell when I was lying anyway, so it wasn't worth trying. Besides that, it would be good to have someone concerned about my well-being and not wanting my bike if I died while I was out getting lost in the wilderness.

"I'm a little bit afraid," I said, quietly. "Not because of backpacking, but mostly because of the unknown. I've never been so high in the mountains before."

"Yes, you have," Summer said, with a smile on her face.

"What a great smile," I thought.

"Remember? Our youth group went to a camp in the mountains a couple of years ago. You were there, Johnny." She stated. She was right!

"Yeah, I do remember now," I said. "But that's not the same. We stayed in nice clean cabins and met in air-conditioned buildings and ate tons of food in their dining hall. This is different. There won't be any cabins or dining halls where we're going. It will be just the three of us hiking on our own. We'll be alone in the wilderness with no one to help us if something happens, or if we get lost."

"You'll know what to do if that happens," she said with confidence. "Remember, you got lost on a hike at that camp two years ago. You told me you totally got turned around, were nervous and scared, but then, you knew just what to do and it all worked out. All you'll need to do is remember what you did last time if something happens to you this time."

"That's right!" I thought. I did get lost on a hike at that camp. I had completely forgotten about that horrible experience. Don't you always try to block bad things like that out of our memory so you'll never have to go through them again? I know I do! Like I try never to think about stuff like my mom's Brussels sprouts, ever! Ugh! Gross!

Ugh! I just thought of them! Gross!

And, just like Brussels sprouts, the memory of that afternoon at camp two years ago gave me a nasty taste in my mouth. I had decided to do a little exploring one day during our afternoon free time. The camp staff had told us not to wander off alone and to always take a hiking buddy with us if we decided to venture out. I would normally have asked Henry or Richie to go with me, but Henry was busy at the pool working on one of his world-famous cannonballs and Richie was searching every corner of the camp to see if he could get any sort of wifi connection.

Camp was where we were supposed to be experiencing nature first-hand. But for Richie, experiencing nature first-hand still meant having contact with the cyber world. There was no being "unplugged" when it came to Richie. If he wanted to really experience a pine tree he would rather source it online, in 3D, HD, and glowing with 10,000 whatever's of color and make it look almost better than the original tree itself.

So, with my two close friends not available as hiking buddies, I figured I would just go a few feet away from the camp, on my own, and catch a little bit of what this God's creation-thing was all about.

I started down a small path and told myself if I could stay on this path I could turn around at any point and walk right back to camp, no problem. I looked around and all I saw was trees and rocks and more trees and rocks and then some trees and rocks. That was all there was out here.

"This is going to get boring fast if things don't pick up a bit!" I thought.

I walked a bit further and nothing much had changed. I was really close to turning around and heading back to camp until I heard something off to my left and away from the trail. It sounded like rushing water. I didn't remember seeing a river when our bus pulled into camp.

"Maybe it's some kind of hidden river, "I thought to myself. "A river no one had ever seen before!"

This needed some exploring, for sure!

I knew I'd have to leave the path a bit to find this mysterious river, or creek or hose left turned on, but I didn't know how far off the path. I didn't want to get lost, so I looked up at the sun to see where it was positioned in the sky. I had seen on TV that sailors and explorers could tell where they were and what direction they were heading by where the sun was in the sky. It was over head and slightly to the right of me. I figured as long as I kept it overhead and slightly to the right of me I could explore, find the mysterious river, name it after myself, and then return to the path, no problem.

So, I stepped off the path, cautiously, and started through the small bushes ahead of me. I looked back every few steps at where the trail was. Then I'd glance up at the sun to make sure it was still in right position. When I felt comfortable that I could easily find my way back to the path, I moved on. I walked between a thick patch of trees and over some rocks but remembered to look up as I did. The sun was still high overhead and slightly to the right. I was good to go on.

"This hiking thing is easy," I thought to myself.

The sound of the rushing water was getting louder with every step so I knew I was close. I took another quick glance at the sun.

"All good."

I walked around a large rock formation where I could hear the sound of the water rushing and, "Boom!" there it was. An awesome stream of water was bursting out of the rocks and sending a waterfall about ten feet down to a small pool below it. The force of the water slamming into the pool made the whole pool churn intensely.

"Awesome!" I shouted. It was an amazing sight! A secret waterfall in a secret place! Maybe it actually was a waterfall no one had ever seen before. Whether it had been discovered before or not, I named it right then and there!

"Welcome to Lazarus Falls!" I shouted proudly...to no one.

I climbed up on a rock next to my namesake waterfall and sat down to get a good view of this amazing sight. I watched as the water continued to fall with great force. An unending supply of powerful water poured and poured over the bank. Spray from the water pounding on the rocks below would hit my face every time the wind changed directions and blew my way. I was hot from my hike, so the spray on my face felt awesome. I closed my eyes and enjoyed the cooling off.

As I sat there with my eyes closed I suddenly felt something tickle my nose. I was not alone like I thought. I opened my eyes immediately, half startled.

"Spider!" I yelled in a panic. "It must be a spider!"

But it wasn't a hairy or scary spider, but instead, the opposite. It was a butterfly. A brightly colored one. It had fluttered in, touched down on my nose while my eyes were closed and then fluttered on. Maybe he was so curious to see someone like me there in the forest, he just had to touch me to see if I was real.

I would never admit it to Henry or Richie or any other guy, because I am a guy, but butterflies were always pretty cool to me, especially this one. It was so colorful I had to stare at it. It was also bold as butterflies go for landing on a human without fear.

"Respect!" I said to him.

I watched him – or her - for a long time as it fluttered around the waterfall. It would flutter close to the water but never too close to be in danger. It knew its limits.

"Respect again!"

Then, joining our party, was a blue jay swooped in and landed on the edge of the river not more than five feet from me.

"Are all the creatures around here this bold?"

It was not only bold but colorful also. Just like the butterfly, it was more colorful than any other blue jay I had ever seen. It was a bright shade of blue, of course, with a shiny black crown of feathers on its head. So regal looking! I could tell it had come to the river for water also and was trying his best to get a drink without getting soaked or knocked in the water by the falls. It knew its limits as well, just like the butterfly.

No, I'm not going to say, "Respect!"

Though he wasn't going to get too close to the water for fear of being swept away he somehow knew I could go in and be strong enough to handle it. How did I know? Because he was looking at me as if to say, "You're this close; you might as well jump in."

Honest! I think he was!

"You're right!" I thought. "Why aren't I jumping in? I'm hot and sweaty from my hike and the water looks refreshing and clean. This looks like fun!"

And with that, I took off my shoes and socks and shirt and jumped in wearing only my shorts. They would probably dry quickly in the warm sun on the way back to camp, so no problem.

When I first stepped in the pool I learned something instantly. Mountain water is cold! Very cold! I almost couldn't breathe because of how cold it was - and almost jumped out! But, I had come this far, so I stayed in and kept my body moving. I let my legs get used to the cold first before going in any deeper, then my upper body and, eventually, all the way to my neck.

"Ahhh! Cold!" I shouted. I could almost hear the butterfly and blue jay laughing.

"Oh really?" I said to them. "Well, then let's see you two get in here!"

Oh man, the cold was getting to me. I was arguing with an insect and a bird!

As I stood there in the cold, my breathing became erratic

and my lower lip began to shiver, but I soon got both under control and excitedly moved towards the waterfall. The spray from it covered me as I got closer and closer. The combination of the warm sun and cold spray was awesome! This was turning out to be one of the greatest moments, if not the greatest, in my life. I couldn't wait to get back to camp and tell Henry, Richie and Summer about this place and bring them here to see *Lazarus Falls!* As adventures go, this one seemed perfect! Perfect, until I happened to glance over at the shore of the river where I had been sitting earlier. I watched in horror as the water from the river surged more than normal, wash up on the rock where my clothes were, grab my shoes, socks and shirt and wash them all down the river.

"Ahhh!" I screamed, "My clothes!"

I couldn't believe my eyes! There they went! Hauled off by the rushing water! There was no way I could catch up with them! They were gone! Gone forever!

This whole adventure had just gone from perfect to a perfect disaster! I would be forced to walk back to camp in only my shorts, cold and barefoot. This was horrible! I only brought one pair of shoes to camp. I would have to go shoeless the rest of the week and have blisters and cuts and gangrene and stuff all over my feet for days.

I slowly climbed out of the river and instantly began to shiver. The warm sun wasn't helping fight off the cold of the mountain stream.

I looked up at the sun and shouted, "A little more heat, please!"

As I stared defiantly at the sun, I noticed something odd. It had moved. It wasn't off to the left a bit or even to the right anymore. It was right on top of me. Straight up! That wasn't where I remembered it. It wasn't where it was *supposed* to be, and certainly not in the position where I knew I could find my way back to the path that lead back to camp. I stared up at it again trying to get my bearings, but it was no good. The sun had moved and now I didn't know where I was or which way to walk.

"Ahhh!" I screamed again!

How was I going to find my way back to camp by following a sun that wasn't where it was supposed to be? How could I follow a sun that was directly on top of me? How does anybody? Wouldn't I just walk around in circles and end up right back where I started? Was I going to be in this one spot for the rest of my life?

"Get it together, Johnny!" I said to myself.

I wasn't going to find my way back to camp by panicking! I'd have to try and figure this out and save myself.

I cleared my head, took a few breaths and thought about what direction to go. I walked a few feet to the left and looked up hoping the sun would be back over to the right where it was supposed to be but it just moved with me. All the sun did no matter which direction I went was follow me and stay on top of me. I walked in the other direction and, same thing. It moved with me. Panic began to creep in again. I was no longer shaking because of the cold. I was shaking out of sheer nervousness about being lost in this forest forever.

"You can do this! You can find that path," I told myself!

I just needed to remember which rock and trees and rock and trees and rock and trees I had seen before.

"I'm doomed!"

I was cold and wet and in BIG trouble.

Chapter 3 Word Study & Doodle on Pages 118-119

# CHAPTER FOUR

## "WET AND WEARY"

"What to do? What to do?" I kept asking myself. I remembered learning when you're lost in the woods, you should stay in one spot and let people find you. Otherwise, you'll probably go the wrong way and get even further lost. I think I learned that in the Boy Scouts or on an episode of Scooby-Doo.

That sounded good in theory, but I wasn't about to sit there in the cold with no shirt or shoes and socks, and freeze to death. I didn't want to become a human Popsicle for a passing bear to munch on. I needed to find the path back to camp and find it quick.

I chose a direction I was pretty sure was back the way I had come from when I left the path to follow the sound to the river. Every step hurt because of my bare feet, but I couldn't worry about that right now. I had to bear whatever pain I had to if I was going to get out of this forest alive. I walked for about five minutes, the same amount of time I had guessed I walked off the path before. But I didn't find the path going in that direction. That scared me and I instinctively called out for people in case I was close enough to the camp to be heard or close enough to the path so maybe a hiker or camper might hear me.

"Hello, anybody out there? Anybody out there smarter than me and who stayed on the path like I should of?" I called out - but I got no response.

In the silence I remember thinking to myself, "I'm all alone out here. No one is going to find me."

But, then something came to mind. I remembered the camp speaker sharing stories from the Bible during our chapel and he read a verse that said God would never leave me or forsake me. I didn't remember what verse it was, but I remember him saying those words. Wow, I actually had listened to the camp speaker!

So, I sat down on a rock near me and looked up, not at the sun this time, but past the sun and up into heaven - and I prayed.

"Lord, I'm in big trouble, again. I know I really only come to you mostly when I'm in big trouble, which is often, so you're probably tired of hearing it from me, but, *this time* I'm in really big trouble. I'm lost, alone, cold, scared and need to find my way back to camp. I don't know which way the camp is, but I know you know everything, so you know the way. If you could get me out of this jam I would totally appreciate it. I know you provide food for the animals of the forest, the bears and mountain lions and wolves, but I'd rather it not be *me* you provided for them this time, okay? I'm pretty sure I wouldn't taste all that great to them anyway. Amen."

I lifted up my head after my prayer and looked all around for a sign from God, but all I saw was rocks and trees and rocks and trees and rocks and trees. They still all looked alike and were spread out in every direction. I was so lost I wasn't sure even God could hear my prayer. I wasn't just lost, I was lost-lost.

"Does God help the lost-lost?" I wondered.

Then the answer came in the strangest of ways. As I stared

at the rocks and trees and rocks and trees I saw something move. It was a butterfly. One that looked just like the one I had seen flutter by the waterfall earlier. It might even be the same one. He fluttered around me and then flew up to my right. As my eyes followed him he passed a branch on the tree next to me and there, sitting calmly, was a blue jay. This blue jay also looked remarkably like the blue jay that had splashed in the waterfall earlier as well. I wondered how long it had been sitting there as I hadn't noticed him until the butterfly flew his direction. The blue jay seemed to look at me and then took off and flew to another branch on a tree about twenty feet away and looked back at me as if to say, "Let's go."

"Are you asking me to follow you, mister blue jay?" I said.

Then it flew to a branch ten feet further away, stopped and looked back at me again. I didn't need to be asked twice. I jumped up and walked towards the bird. Every time I got close to him, he would fly to another branch on a tree up ahead and, of course, I followed. Branch after branch he went and step by step I followed.

"I hope you're leading me to safety and not some bear's cave," I said. "Are you the bluebird of happiness or a bear's evil henchman?"

Being disoriented must have started to get to me. I was having a conversation with a blue jay about his agenda. I continued to follow him though and, at one point, instead of flying forward, he left the branch he was on and flew straight up towards the sky and disappeared into the glare of the sun. I had to close my eyes so I wouldn't stare directly into it.

"Oh, no!" I thought. "He's gone!" My hiking buddy had flown the coop! "What am I going to do now?"

As I stared at the ground in despair I suddenly realized something. I was standing on a path. And, not just any path, but the path back to camp! It had to be! The blue jay had somehow returned me to safety! I could barely believe it! I started sprinting back in the direction I had come from before! I was stepping on rocks and gravel and twigs with my bare feet but I never really felt any pain! I was too excited to know I'd been rescued!

I eventually saw the edge of the camp and ran even faster to get there. I came out of the woods in full stride and right into the middle of the grass field where tons of campers were playing games. Instantly, when they saw me run in, they all stopped what they were doing to look at the shirtless, shoeless, wet, dirty, scraped up weirdo run by. I must have looked like Tarzan, as a boy, entering a village and encountering man for the first time. I stared back and didn't say anything. I was just so glad to be safe.

Henry and Richie jumped off a low-ropes course they were playing on and ran over to meet me. They looked me up and down for a few seconds and then Henry finally said something.

"You obviously have been having more fun than we have!"

"What's with the jungle boy look, Johnny?" Richie asked. "What awesome activity did you find that we didn't hear about?"

"Guys!" I said, interrupting Richie. "I wasn't doing any activity. I nearly died in the forest just now!"

"Oh, really? How?" Henry said with an unbelieving voice.

"I went for a hike on one of the hiking paths and got lost.

"How did you get lost on a path?" Richie asked.

"Because I broke hiking rules one and two," I said. "I didn't take a hiking buddy with me because you guys were too busy and I left the path I was hiking on.

"Left the path?" Henry shouted. "You never leave the path! Nothing good ever happens when you leave the path!"

"Usually not," I said.

Richie stared at me and then asked, "What do you mean, *usually* not, Johnny"

I leaned to both of them and whispered, "I found something cool. Something in the forest I don't think anyone has even seen before and it's awesome!

"What?" Henry shouted!

"Shhhh!" I said, looking around. "Keep it down, Henry!"

"Sorry, Johnny, but you know I don't like not knowing things! I've got to know what others know, you know that! So, tell me what you know so I'll know because you know I've got to know!

I could see Henry was starting to lose it! Henry couldn't stand being left out of anything. He had to be a part of the inner circle of things or it drove him crazy. Sometimes, I would let him stir for a bit and not share stuff with him right away. It was fun to watch him slowly go bonkers, but what I had found this time couldn't wait, and it looked like Henry couldn't wait either. So, I filled them in on my great discovery.

"I found a hidden waterfall deep in the forest," I whispered, "and a mysterious river that would lure you into it and then grab your shoes and socks and shirt and haul them away!"

"A river that steals?" Richie said, not believing me. "Come on, Johnny."

"Why do you think I'm standing here with just my shorts on?" I asked. "Because the rest of my clothes are gone - taken by that evil river - never to be seen again! I think the river was trying to protect its secrecy and the only way to do that was to make sure I never returned to tell the tale!"

Richie still stared at me in disbelief, but Henry hoped I might be telling the truth. This would make a great story he could

41

share back home. Sharing great stories like mine or a classic Coastal Eddie adventure made Henry popular at school. He was a masterful storyteller and had a way of making tales bigger than life! Kids would give up their entire lunch period just to hear him share. So, he was in the market for some good summer material that he could use to draw a crowd when we went back to school in the Fall.

"Wow!" Henry said. "How did you eventually make it back here, Johnny?"

"When I saw the river grab my clothes and run I immediately climbed out of the water and began to wonder what I was going to do. I was cold, scared and lost because the sun had moved on me taking away my sense of direction. I tried walking in the direction that I thought would get me back on the path to camp but I just got more lost and confused. I couldn't find my way back! That was, until a butterfly and blue jay I met told me to follow them and led me back to the path and back to camp. Honest."

"Whoa, whoa! Clothes stealing waterfalls? Butterflies and blue jays giving out directions?" Richie questioned in disgust. "What kind of fools do you think we are, Johnny?"

"I know it sounds weird, but that's what happened!"

"Then we need to tell someone about this." Richie stated.

"Who?" Henry asked.

"The camp nurse!" Richie said. "Because it's obvious Johnny's got a serious case of sunstroke or something."

"Maybe you ate some plant out there and it drugged you and you just imagined all this, Johnny." Henry said, sympathetically.

"Hello, jungle boy. My name is Mr. Butterfly and this is my best friend, Mr. Bluejay. Can we talk?" Richie quipped. And with that, Henry and Richie went running back to the ropes course laughing.

"Me Tarzan, you coo-coo!" Henry shouted at me as they ran away.

"I didn't have sunstroke or eat some strange plant, I don't think? This really happened, didn't it?"
I thought for a second and then shouted, "Yes, it did!"

I walked back to my cabin knowing kids were staring at me but I didn't look up, I just kept walking. I grabbed my towel, shampoo, fresh clothes and a pair of sandals I brought to wear to the pool and headed for the shower.

Once I was cleaned up and back in my cabin, I climbed up on my bunk and stared at the roof of the cabin. I had been through the adventure of a lifetime and it was so bizarre that no one would ever believe me. Hidden waterfalls, butterflies, blue jays? It did sound crazy. But, I knew it was true and I knew someone else who knew it was true - God.

"Thank you for saving me, God. Thank you for sending help in whatever form when I asked."

I wasn't completely sure if that was how God actually worked or if the whole thing was one big coincidence. All I knew was I asked to be rescued and God came through. I reached under my pillow and grabbed my Bible. I opened it to the lesson the camp speaker had shared earlier that day and found that Scripture I remembered in the forest. It was Deuteronomy 31:8

*"The Lord himself goes before you and will be with you; He will never leave you nor forsake you."*

I took a pen out and underlined it. I now knew this to be truer than anything I had ever read, ever.

I stayed on my bunk for awhile and read a few more verses

in Deuteronomy.

"This is the coolest book in the Bible!" I thought. "Because it has the word *dude* in it!"

"Dude-eronomy!" I said out loud a few times and laughed.

"What are you laughing about, Johnny?" Summer said, waking me up from my camping daydream - or nightmare.

"Oh, um, I'm laughing about getting lost at camp two years ago," I said, "and how ridiculous my explanation sounded to Henry and Richie back then. The way I found my way back to camp, that is."

"You know, you never really told me how you made it back to camp that day, Johnny." She said.

"Trust me, Summer, if I told you how I got back you'd think I was wacko! Everyone would. Henry and Richie thought so even though I told them it was not a lie! They just laughed at me, so I just stopped talking about it. It will just have to go down as the Big Dude's, I mean, God's and my little secret."

"Wow, you and God share secrets, Johnny? I sure like that in a man," Summer said with a smile on her face.

And, with that, she hopped up and started walking towards her house.

She looked back and with a clever voice and said, "I like that in a boy, too! I think it helps keep them focused. It helps him find the best *path* for his life."

"Path? Who told you about the path?" I asked, feeling that funny feeling I always felt when I was around her.

"Oh, let's just say a little birdie told me," she said, and she walked in her house.

"Path? Birdie? Who are you, Summer Breeze?"

Chapter 4 Word Study & Doodle on Pages 120-121

# CHAPTER FIVE
## "LEFT OUT IN THE COLD!"

The big day had finally arrived. My dad, my brother Steve and I were about to scale a huge mountain and try to survive in the wild for three whole days with only the stuff we were carrying on our backs. My mom drove us to the site, and, as we got closer, my dad pointed out the mountain we were about to climb. It looked even bigger than I had imagined.

"Are you sure we can make it to the top of that huge thing and then get back down to earth safely." I asked to no one in particular.

"If not," my brother said, "we'll just have to leave those who can't handle it behind, right dad?"

"We can't have any dead weight holding us back, so if we need to cut someone loose, for the sake of the rest, we'll have to do it!" My dad said.

"What?" I said with a panic.

My dad and my brother just started laughing. Even my mom joined in.

"No one is getting left behind, Johnny," my mom said.

"You would be missed so much if you didn't come home."

"Yeah, I mean, who would we have to put out the trash

every week if you weren't there?" My dad said, and they all laughed again.

"Not funny!" I said sternly. "Not funny at all!"

We finally pulled into a parking lot at the base of the mountain. There were a couple of other cars with people unloading backpacking gear as well. Were we going in a group? I thought my dad said it was just going to be the three of us.

Dad unloaded our packs out of the back of the car while I stretched my legs from the long drive. Then my dad went over and talked to a couple of the other dads there. When he came back I asked him if all these other people were going with us. He told me no. There were about five or six different trails that began from this point but none of our groups were taking the same trail.

"They are all doing the easier loops on the trail," my dad said as he returned to the car. "We are the only ones doing 'The Monster,' as they call it."

"The Monster?" I said, with noticeable fear in my voice. "I don't like the sound of that!"

"Ooh, is my wittle brudder afwaid of the big bad monster mountain?" My brother asked in his humiliating baby talk.

"I'm not afwaid, I mean, afraid of anything!" I announced!

To prove it, I walked over, grabbed my backpack and said, "Let's do this thing!" And, with that, I lifted my backpack up onto my shoulders! Or at least I tried - but there was a problem. It wouldn't budge from the ground. I couldn't lift it, not at first. I tried again, with all my might, and barely got it up to my waist before having to set it down again. Was there some kind of gravitational pull here I didn't know about? I repositioned myself, trying not to look like I was trying too hard and lifted again. It took all my strength and a boost from my dad to finally get a strap over one shoulder, but then I had to put it back down on the ground again. It landed with a thud.

"What's wrong, Johnny?" my dad said as he and my brother both lifted and put their backpacks on with no problem.

"Someone's playing a trick on me," I said, staring at my brother. "My pack is way too heavy to lift. Steve must have stuffed it with lead or something!"

My mom walked over and reached for my backpack. Then she lifted it with no problem. How embarrassing!

"It's fine, Johnny," my mom said. "Come over here and I'll help you put it on."

She continued to hold it high in the air without much trouble while I walked over. "Was my mom a superhero in disguise?" I thought to myself.

I put one arm in a strap and then the other. My mom then let the weight of the backpack fall onto my shoulders. It weighed a ton and I felt my legs start to buckle! Pain shot through my legs but everyone was staring at me, so I hid the fact that my legs were burning. I couldn't let them see that this backpack was so heavy I couldn't move. Especially after my mom had just "clean and jerked" the backpack off the ground with ease, like some Russian Olympic weightlifter. Obviously, when I filled my backpack at home to practice backpacking I totally underestimated how much I would be carrying - by about a hundred pounds, it felt like.

"Are we good to go?" My dad said.

"Good to go!" My brother hollered out.

"How about you, Johnny." My dad said as he gave my mom a hug.

"G-good to go!" I said, with a fake smile on my face.

"Good to go home and forget this whole thing!" I said

49

under my breath.

And, with a hug from my mom and a wave of my dad's hand we started out of the parking lot and onto the trail. I should have said something. I knew for a fact I couldn't complete this journey, but I stayed silent. My pride kept me quiet, for now. We walked down the path and into the forest ready to take on "The Monster."

"Lord, help me!"

My legs were feeling the weight of my pack with every step and I grew tired quickly. I was struggling with every step and we hadn't even started going up yet. We were still just walking on the part of the trail that would take us closer to the base of the mountain.

How was I going to be able to keep this up for three days? I wasn't sure, but I knew it would involve having to stop, many times.

"That's it!" I said to myself. "I'll make sure we take a bunch of breaks along the way!"

I began devising a plan to help with my strategy.

"Hey, dad, I think we're walking too fast." I said, hoping he might stop for a minute.

"Too fast? We have a lot of ground to cover in this first day, so we need to set a good pace," He said. "Are you having trouble keeping up? I know you practiced a lot at home this week."

"He's going to wimp out, I just know it," my brother said with disgust in his voice. "Wimpy, wimpy, whmpy."

" No, no, I don't mean too fast to handle it, I just mean too fast to see all of God's beauty around us. We are missing all the nature and birds and plants and stuff because we're walking right past it." I was laying it on pretty thick and knew I was lying but my legs were growing weaker with every step and my back was starting to ache. "Can we stop and take it all in occasionally? I don't want to miss anything."

"We'll stop at certain points, Johnny, but only after we've put in a good amount of walking," my dad said.

"We've done a good amount so far, haven't we?" I asked. "I mean, we've been walking forever!"

"Forever?" My brother said. "You can still see the parking lot from here!"

I turned around and could see our car in the distance and my mom waving at us. How embarrassing!

Step after step after step, everyone more painful than the last, I just stared at the ground and kept going. I looked down so I wouldn't see how far we still had to go and, also, I wanted to be sure if my leg fell off I'd know about it. I was getting tired and thirsty and sore and discouraged all at the same time. Suddenly, my pity-party was interrupted by a shout from my dad.

"Great news, boys!" He shouted.

"The mountain is closed for repairs?" I hoped.

"We are at the base of the mountain! We can start climbing now!" He said with actual joy in his voice.

I finally looked up for the first time in awhile and my dad was right. Right in front of us was the mountain.

"Hello, Mr. Monster!" I said to myself. "Feeding time should be in about an hour! Devour me quickly, please."

The trail from there seemed to veer off to the left and went upward at an angle. I didn't like the look of that. Flatland had beaten me up pretty good so I knew too much climbing would be the knockout blow that finished me off.

51

You know that part in a mystery on TV where someone goes missing and the police find their diary in their room and on the last page of the last day they wrote something and there is only half an entry? The writing just stops mysteriously leaving everyone baffled? This would be that day for me - if I kept a diary – but I don't. So, my disappearance will probably go unresolved. No one will ever really know what happened to me especially if my dad and brother, Steve, have to eat me to survive. They won't be talking.

"Good-bye, cruel world!" I said under my breath, and with that we started up the mountain.

The incline made my knees start to ache, but that took my attention off my back pain, so I kept going. We walked about forty or fifty feet and then, all of a sudden, we turned and began walking in the other direction. Still on an incline and still climbing, but now I could see below me the trail we had just walked on.

"Dad, why did we change directions like that?" I asked.

"Was the guy who made this trail confused about where he was going and have to make a sudden turn?"

"No, Johnny," my dad said. "These are called switchbacks. These make it easier to ascend the mountain without having to go straight up. They make the journey much longer, but it pays off in the end because going straight up would be near impossible."

"Make the journey much longer?" I questioned under my breath. "Note to diary I don't have. This Mr. Switchback is now the key suspect of my demise."

I soon began to count the switchbacks as we completed them, one by one. Partly to make the time pass quicker, and partly so I would remember how many I had to cover to get out of here at the end of three days. I was sweating up a storm. It was getting hotter and hotter as the day went on and I could now add the discomfort of walking in the mountain wearing jeans to my list of reasons I would probably never do this backpacking-thing again. My dad made us wear jeans because he said they were durable, would help prevent bug bites and unnecessary scrapes. I figured doing it to torture us was in there somewhere, too.

After an hour or more of hiking my mouth was dry. I could use a drink of water in a bad way, which reminded me of something. Our backpacking clip-cups! I had forgotten all about them because of focusing on the excruciating pain instead.

One of the great things we got to go with our backpacks, if there was such a thing was our cool backpacking clip-cup. It was a metal drinking cup with a clip on it so we could hook it to our belt buckle and have it at the ready at all times to scoop up water without having to hold onto it while we hiked. I had it clipped to my left side belt buckle just like my brother and my dad. My dad had showed us how they worked and how quickly you could take it off your belt loop and put it back on, sometimes without even looking. My brother and I practiced every day to see which of us could take it off and put it back on faster. Kind of like a cowboy pulls his gun as fast as he can from his holster in a gun fight. I had even challenged my brother a few times at home to see if I could outdraw him. I lost every time. Remember, he was better than me at everything. Why not clip-cups?

Of course, none of those practice losses mattered now! This was the real deal and I was really thirsty. He would not outdraw me this time if even the smallest drop of water showed itself. This town wasn't big enough for two thirsty hikers!

"Dad, my mouth is drying up! I need some water!" I said with a scratchy voice.

"Good timing," my dad said. "According to our map, there

is supposed to be a small mountain creek up ahead. Nothing tastes better than fresh, cold, clean mountain water. Melting snow is God's drinking fountain!"

Melting snow sounded good to me. I was hot, sweaty and parched. I could jump into a pile of cold snow right now.

We turned to head up another switchback. Number forty five or forty six, I had lost count – but just then I heard it – the faint sound of running water. The creek was near. I went for my clip-cup as fast as I could and snatched it off my belt in record time. My brother was already holding his and looked at me with a nasty grin. The young whipper-snapper had won again.

We followed the sound of the trickling water and as it got louder we knew we were close. My brother spotted it first and pointed. I looked over and saw it too. It looked awesome! When you were as hot and tired and thirsty as I was, it could have just been an old hose with holes in it hanging from a fence and still looked awesome! But this was no hose! This was a real live mountain stream and it was calling me!

As we got closer you could see the water pouring down off a rock and making a waterfall that landed in a small pool. We both headed for the pool to scoop up some water, but my dad stopped us.

"Don't drink the still water; scoop the rushing water from the creek. That's the fresh stuff!"

So, we walked over to where the water was trickling down a path making a creek about three feet wide. Water was bouncing off of rocks and rushing past us. It looked so inviting I couldn't wait. I reached down to scoop up a clip-cup full of this mountain goodness completely forgetting I had a forty pound backpack on my back. As I leaned down I never stopped! I just kept going down and down! The weight of the backpack kept pushing me downward until it plunged me into the creek! I landed face-first in it soaking the entire front of me with ice cold water. I gasped for air and struggled to try and get up but my backpack was so heavy it held me down in the freezing water. I could feel the wet and cold soaking through my shirt, my pants - my everything! I had been in cold water before but this was the coldest ever. It was so cold it took my breath away for a second.

I struggled to turn my head to the side and yell for help. I could see my brother standing next to me but he wasn't doing anything to help me. He was too busy laughing. He told me later that day it was probably one of the top five funniest things he had ever seen in his life.

"Your backpack was trying to drown you! It was hilarious!" He said.

"Really funny," I said to him. "I'm drowning and you're rating it on your humor scale."

My dad finally ran over and grabbed my backpack lifting it and me up from the creek and back onto my feet. I was shivering from the cold and probably from the fear of thinking I was about to die.

"What were you doing, Johnny?" My dad asked.

"I w-w-was t-trying to get a d-drink of w-water," I struggled to say with my lips quivering frantically.

"Well, that was quite a drink," my brother said with a laugh.

"We're close to where we're going to set up camp for the first night, so we'll walk there and then we can change out of your wet clothes," my dad said. "It might be bit uncomfortable to walk in wet clothes but we're not far from our first stop."

*Uncomfortable* wasn't the word for it. Have you ever tried walking in wet jeans? Jeans were never meant to be walked in while wet, especially when you're climbing a mountain and have a giant backpack on your back. With every step I took I could feel the wet jeans scraping across my legs. It felt like they were ripping the skin off with every step. I was now wet, cold, tired, sore and my legs were stinging like a nasty sunburn. I made a vow right then and there that, if I ever had kids of my own, I would do them the biggest favor ever and never ever force them to go backpacking...or wear jeans.

Chapter 5 Word Study & Doodle on Pages 122-123

# CHAPTER SIX

## "GOD'S COUNTRY"

"We camp here," my dad said stopping on the trail.

I don't think I had ever heard three better words in my life. So far my first (and only if I had anything to say about it) backpacking experience consisted of an aching back, sore shoulders, legs that were worn out and chaffed from being assaulted by wet jeans. I was cold, tired, wet, hungry and angry. Angry my dad ever came up with such a dumb idea as this. I wanted to be off this mountain and home in my bed right now. I pictured myself snuggled up with a pillow safe and warm in my favorite pajamas. Not high in the mountains on a dusty trail in wet clothes and freezing to death.

"This ground here is almost level and these rocks will make for great pillows. It will be the perfect place to sleep tonight," my dad said.

"Ahhhh!" I screamed. I couldn't hold it in anymore! I had to let it all out! All the anger and frustration! All the hurt and cold! All the - *everything!*

"What's wrong, Johnny?" My dad said.

"What's wrong?" I shouted. "What's right? I want to go home, now! This was a bad idea from the start! Making me walk up a mountain carrying a backpack that weighs as much as I do! Almost drowning in ice cold water while my brother laughs in my face! Switchback after stinking switchback and now a rock for a pillow? Where is the fun in any of this? You told me it might be tough but the reward would be worth it. Well, I'm not seeing any reward, dad! Show me the reward!"

I was practically crying by the time I finished ranting. My dad listened and then calmly said, "Have you looked at the sunset behind you?"

A sunset! A dumb sunset! Was that the best he could do? I was in a state of misery and all he was offering me was a sunset? I wanted to yell more but thought my dad might just calmly tell me to look at a flower or something. I stared at him and my brother but they weren't looking back at me. They were both staring over my shoulder and their faces were turning orange. I turned around defiantly. I was ready to glance at the sunset and then begin pity-party number two but, I was stopped in mid-pity by the sky behind me – and the sunset.

I had seen plenty of pretty good sunsets growing up, especially because we lived at the beach. But, what I saw before me right now was more than just a pretty good sunset. It was amazing! It was more than amazing! It was "forget about your pain, your cold and your anger" amazing!

There was a light show going on in the sky like I had never seen before. Light was blasting colors in every direction. The sky had been transformed into a giant canvas with streaks of bright colors covering every inch of it. I just stood there in awe. We all did. Even my brother was impressed, which was hard to do.

"Man!" Steve said which was exactly what I was thinking.

"No, God!" My dad followed with. "This is God's handywork. No one can paint the sky or anything like He can."

The brilliance of the sunset was indescribable. There were colors in it I had never seen in the sunsets back home or anywhere before. It was truly awesome! It even made me forget about not wanting to be there. It seemed to warm me up and heal my body all at the same time.

"You still want to go home?" My dad asked.

"Um, maybe I'll give backpacking one more day," I said sheepishly, and I sat down right where I was and continued to stare at the sky.

My dad cleared an area for us, got our mats and sleeping bags positioned and pulled out a small stove, a pot and the dehydrated food pouches we were supposed to eat for meal one. He called Steve and me over to watch how he started the fire on the small stove so we would know how to do it later on. He told us we would each have a turn preparing a meal so we should learn what to do. Then he put the pot on the burner and filled it with water from a canteen he was carrying.

"As soon as the water boils," he said, "we'll add in the food from the pouch and let it cook until done."

He showed us the food pouch which read, "Mac and Cheese" which sounded awesome at that moment. Nothing can cure what ails you like Mac and Cheese. My brother and I dug into our backpacks and pulled out our metal backpacking bowls and a fork. We couldn't wait.

The sunset slowly began to lose its brilliance as the sun began to go behind the mountain range on the other side of the valley. It also started to get colder. I had changed out of my wet clothes by now and into dry stuff but still had to put on my jacket to try and stay warm.

"How much longer on the Mac and Cheese, dad?" I asked.

"Any minute now," he said, and said, and said, for about thirty minutes. We kept waiting for the water to boil but it never did. There were bubbles forming on the bottom of the pot but they never bubbled up to the surface. The water wouldn't boil no matter how much my dad turned up the heat on the small stove.

"It must be the thin air up here this high in the mountains. It won't let the water boil," my dad said, staring in the pot.

"What are we going to do? I'm starving!" My brother said.

"We've waited long enough and nothing's happening, so let's give it a shot," my dad said with some reluctance.

He then grabbed the Mac and Cheese packet, tore it open and poured the powdered food into the water.

He was hoping the water might be just hot enough to turn the yellow dust into something edible, which it didn't. The powder did change, but not to a smooth and tasty looking Mac and Cheese. It became more of a yellowish goo somewhere between paste and chalk.

"Dig in," my dad said and he scooped some onto his plate.

He looked at it for a second and then he took a big bite of the stuff. We watched as he choked down the first bite and went right to his water. My brother and I were so hungry we took turns scooping yellow globs into our bowls and looking at each other as if to say, "Are we really going to do this?"

The first bite I took tasted about as nasty as the Mac and Cheese looked and I almost barfed it back up! But, I was so hungry and it was all we had, so I kept going. There were some clumps in it that were part chewy and part crunchy depending on which clump you chose. The faces my brother and I made with each bite announced to each of us that what we tasted was as nasty as it looked. We scooped, ate, drank water and swallowed as fast as we could, repeatedly, until it was all gone. The only thing good about the yellow goo was that it was filling and my hunger actually went away.

When we finished my dad put me in charge of taking our dishes over to the river and washing them out. We would each take a turn as dishwasher for a meal. I gathered up everything and headed for a stream a few feet away. The moon had replaced the sun and it was shining bright in the sky. It made a cool reflection on the water of the creek. It also lit up the night enough so I could see what I was doing. In the middle of washing the last dish I noticed something in the water next to me that startled me. As I looked closer I could see it was a fish - probably a trout. It was just sitting there no more than ten feet away from the shore and it was staring at me. He was only about a foot deep in the water and appeared to be watching my every movement. Almost like he was making sure I was doing a good job cleaning the dishes.

"You don't want to eat this stuff," I said to him, jokingly. He didn't laugh.

I couldn't wait to tell my dad and brother what I had seen. If that big trout was there in the morning, we weren't going to have to choke down half-cooked, powder-goo. We'd be having fresh trout grilled over an open flame!

When I got back to camp my dad and brother had already set everything up for sleeping the first night. Dad had also thrown a rope over a nearby tree and hoisted our food into the air so bears and other animals couldn't get at it. I figured there wasn't going to be any problem with animals wanting our food. It tasted nasty!

"Dad!" I shouted. "You're not going to believe what I saw in the river!"

"A pizza deliveryman I hope," my brother said sarcastically.

"No, I saw a trout! A *huge* one and it was only a few feet away from me! I could tell it was hungry! It was staring me down and hoping I had brought him something good to eat. Unfortunately, I only had the leftover Mac and Goo! But tomorrow I *will* have something he'll want to chomp on and when he does we'll be eating in style for breakfast! Leave out the frying pan, dad. That bad boy will be on my hook by sunrise!" I exclaimed.

"Sounds good, Johnny! I can't wait!" My dad said excitedly. "We all better get some sleep if we're going to be up that early."

You didn't have to tell me twice about getting some sleep. I was so tired from hiking I knew I'd be out cold the minute my head hit the pillow – uh, rock.

We all took off our shoes and climbed into our sleeping bags. We were lined up next to each other and we were all lying on our backs looking up at the night sky. I shifted back and forth trying to get the ground under me to move in a way that would feel comfortable. I could hear my dad and Steve shifting around also. The ground wasn't soft, at all, but it was flat enough to lie on. Once we settled in we all stared up at the moon which looked bigger and brighter than any moon I had ever seen it before. Just like the sunset earlier was more amazing than back at home, the moon was more amazing, too.

"I can see a face clearly in the moon," I said as I looked up.

"Maybe that's God looking down on us and letting us know we're not alone," my dad said.

"Maybe He's guarding our campsite so no critters bother

64

us," I said.

"Maybe that's just shadows in its craters and you are both a couple of dorks," my brother said, and we all laughed.

I was right about falling asleep quickly. I was so worn out I dozed off in only a few minutes. Hard bed or not my body was wanting, no, craving rest. I dreamed that night of catching that trout and winning the award for catching the largest trout in the world. Even bigger than the one my brother caught. Steve only got third place this time. I had finally beaten him at something! I had finally done something better than him!

A guy can dream, can't he?

Chapter 6 Word Study & Doodle on Pages 124-125

# CHAPTER SEVEN

# "FISH OUT OF WATER!"

When I awoke the next morning the sun was already coming over the mountainside. My dad had cooked some powdered eggs that actually looked like and, surprisingly, tasted like scrambled eggs. I smothered them with ketchup from some pouches we brought, just in case. You can't eat scrambled eggs without ketchup. I knew that and my dad knew that, so he threw a few packs in.

It took a bit of time for me to realize my brother wasn't there. I was still sleepy and too focused on the eggs.

"Where is Steve?" I asked. "A bear didn't haul him away in the middle of the night, did he?" I hoped not. I didn't want to have to carry his part of the load on the rest of the trip. Oh, and I cared about his safety a bit, too.

"He ate breakfast quickly and then grabbed the fishing gear and headed over to the river where you said you saw that big trout," my dad said.

"What?!" I shouted. "He's going to catch my fish! No fair! No fair! How could you let him do that, dad! That is my fish! I'm supposed to win the contest this time, not Steve!"

"Contest," My dad questioned? "Remember, Johnny, you

might have seen that trout first, but it's nobody's fish until someone catches it. That's the law of fishing."

I was pretty sure there was no such law like that. This was just another one of my dad's speeches to keep me from going ballistic. He could tell when I was *ballistic-mad* and he always tried to defuse me before I exploded. Sometimes it worked, but not this time! If my brother had caught my fish, speech or no speech, all you were going to hear on this mountain was a loud Ka-Boom!

I put on my shoes in record time, grabbed my fishing gear and ran for the river as fast as I could. Hopefully, my brother hadn't landed that big boy yet. Law, or no law, in my mind I saw it first, so that fish was mine!

When I got there my brother had his line in the water and I thought I could hear him talking to himself. When I got closer I realized he wasn't talking to himself, he was talking to my fish.

"What more do you want, you dumb fish?" He said with disgust. "That's almost all the cheese I have! Eat it already!"

I looked in the water where my brother was staring and could see a big trout just staring back at him. It had to be the one I saw the night before. He had that same smirk on his face as last night. My brother had his line in the water right in front of Tommy the Trout (I named it) with a giant piece of cheese on his hook and it was dangling right in front of Tommy's nose, if fish had noses. But Tommy showed no interest in it. He just looked at it as if to say, "Don't you have anything better than this. Don't you have a *better-cheddar?*"

Seeing that my brother hadn't caught Tommy and that it didn't appear he was going to calmed me down a bit.

"Maybe he wants a little wine with his cheese," I said with a laugh. My brother didn't laugh back.

"He doesn't want anything," my brother said. "I've tried bread, a lure, salmon eggs and now this cheese - and nothing! Not even a hint of being interested."

It appeared my "great at everything" brother had finally met his match. He reeled in his line, grabbed his gear and headed back to camp.

"Don't waste your time on this fish, Johnny," Steve said as he walked away. "If I can't catch it, no one can."

He was probably right, but I didn't like how it made me feel, so I had to try. Just because he had failed didn't automatically mean I would. This was my one chance to outdo him.

"Tell dad to keep the frying pan warm!" I shouted at Steve as he walked away.

"Yeah, right!" My brother said without looking back.

Well, here it was. I had been given another opportunity to beat him at something and I needed to take advantage of it. I needed to catch this fish even if I had to go into the water after it myself.

"Wait! I take that back!" I said looking down at my second and only other pair of jeans. "I'm not getting these babies anywhere close to water! I'm not going through that again!"

I backed a foot or so away from the water just to be safe. I went into my fishing gear and took out my jar of salmon eggs. They were bright pink and looked like little jelly beans to me.

"Who could refuse a jelly bean," I thought, and I put a couple of them on my hook. I took aim carefully and then cast my line Tommy's way. A perfect shot about a foot in front of him. I know he saw it and would go for it at any minute – which turned into thirty minutes – and not a bite. I spent the whole time trying everything to get Tommy interested in biting my hook. He just sat there and stared at me but never budged.

I began to talk to him much like my brother did earlier.

"Are you fasting or something, Tommy?" I asked. "Is this some kind of spiritual time for you?"

I explained to Tommy how much of a hero he would be to me by letting me catch him and that his ultimate sacrifice would not be in vain. Nothing! I offered to take pictures of him and post him all over Facebook and Instagram and even do a feature of him on YouTube if he came back to camp with me. Nothing!

"Do you have an older brother, Tommy?" I asked. "Do you know how inferior they make us younger brothers feel? We need to fight back, Tommy! Bite the hook! For younger brothers throughout the world who want to be better than their older brothers at something, please, bite the hook!"

Zilch, nada, nothing! He never moved. I continued to plead, beg and even threaten him as if he could understand me. Nothing! He just sat there.

Pretty soon a second trout swam up next to him and just stood there staring at me, too. Tommy turned his head and looked at him as if to say, "This is one of the jokers I've been telling you about." Bubbles came out of their mouths that I took to be laughing. How embarrassing!

When the bubbles subsided, which took awhile, I realized I had been there too long, and nothing was going to work anyway, so I reeled in my line, gathered everything up and started back to camp.

"Thanks for nothing!" I said to Tommy as I walked away. He didn't hear me though. He was too busy chewing on a big piece of cheese I pulled off my hook and threw at him - of course.

"Glad you're back, Johnny. Let's hit the trail for day two," my dad said as I entered our campsite. Dad had cleaned up everything and had my pack ready to go.

"Thanks for the vote of confidence," I thought to myself.

He didn't even wait to see if I would catch that trout. Probably decided if my brother couldn't catch it, it was uncatchable. I decided right then and there I would show them both who could or couldn't do something the best. I was going to blaze the trail that day and leave them both in the dust!

"Call me Johnny Trailblazer!" I said as I went for my pack.

I grabbed my backpack with newfound confidence and hoisted it on to my back. I was hoping it would feel a lot lighter without the Mac and Cheese I had been carrying the day before, but no such luck. When I lifted my backpack I realized it wasn't any lighter, at all. In fact, it felt heavier than before and my legs started to ache before I had even taken one step! I wondered if my brother had slipped some of his stuff into my pack while I was gone, but it only felt heavier because of how tired and sore I was from hiking the day before.

"Woo-Hoo, Day two!" I shouted as we started out. My dad thought I was saying it because I was excited to backpack again. I was, however, really saying it to hide the pain I was feeling and because it also meant once this day was over there would only be one more day to go. I couldn't wait for this trip to end. The incredible sunset yesterday and the giant moon last night were awesome but they became distant memories the minute we hit the first switchback.

"If I ever run into this Jim Switchback-guy, or whoever it was who invented these switchback-things, I'm going to kick him in the shins - if I can ever lift my foot that high again."

**We hiked** long and hard for another day stopping only to

have lunch and to fill up our canteens which I did every time we met up with the stream that seemed to be following us through the mountain. It would appear and then disappear for awhile as if it was playing hide and seek with us. Sometimes I could hear it but not see it and sometimes I couldn't hear it at all but it would be around the bend waiting for me.

Each time we passed the stream, I began to notice something about it. It was growing. It was slowly getting stronger and wider in size. At one point I figured it had to be twice as wide as before and it was rushing more swiftly and powerfully than any time before. It had to be a good fifteen to twenty feet across at its widest point and you could now feel the spray coming off of it everywhere it slammed against big rocks along its edge. The spray felt great on my face which, like always, had become hot and sweaty from all that hiking.

My dad jumped up on a rock and started singing, "Old man river! That old man river! He just keeps rolling along!"

"Oh, great!" I said to Steve. "Dad's brain has finally snapped!"

"If he keeps this up we'll push him in the Old Man River and watch him just keep rolling along," Steve said and we laughed until my dad had done a few more choruses about cotton and whatever.

He finally stopped. Steve and I applauded. Dad bowed, almost lost his pack and we moved on. Crisis averted – for now.

The second night was much like the first except my dad actually got the water on the tiny stove to boil. We were at a much lower elevation on the mountain than the night before because we were actually moving downward and that meant the air wasn't as thin. We ate powdered chili that cooked up kind of great and tasted pretty good. We broke up some crackers dad had packed and threw those in the chili along with the last of our chunks of cheese. Less for Tommy the Trout meant more for us!

"Not bad, dad," I said scooping a spoonful of chili into my mouth.

"Thanks," my dad said. "See, I knew you two would like backpacking once you got into it."

"Uh, I just said the chili was good, dad," I reminded him. "I think I've said it a few times. I'm never going backpacking again!"

"You've said it a hundred!" My brother commented.

"Never say never, son," dad said. "You still have one more day to test it out and then you can decide. There could be something incredible waiting just around the corner that might change your mind."

"It would have to be something huge like an In and Out Burger, or a giant hotel with a massive room and a hot shower," I said. "Oh, and the biggest bed with the fluffiest pillow in the whole world, and a big trout, that I caught, named Tommy roasting on a grill!"

"Stop dreaming and give me your dishes so I can clean them or I'll roast you on a grill!" My brother barked.

I had to laugh because that was funny. It's funny how Steve can make me so mad at times and then turn around and make me laugh the hardest also. Sometimes I think he wants to pound me and other times I know he'd protect me no matter what. Sometimes I didn't want him near me or I didn't even want to see his face and other times he was the best person to have around. This was one of those times. Brothers can be the cruelest and brothers can be the coolest. You take the good with the bad because you need each other and know you still love each other I guess.

We slept under the bright moon for the second night with that same smiling face looking down on us. Yes, I knew it was just shadows from the craters on its surface like my brother said, but I still thought of it as a person placed there to protect me.

"Good night, Mr. Moon." I said so no one could hear me.

"Good night, dork!" My brother said. He could hear me.

Embarrassed, again.

Chapter 7 Word Study & Doodle on Pages 126-127

# CHAPTER EIGHT
## "AND A RIVER RUNS THROUGH IT"

I sprang out of bed the next morning feeling better than I had the entire trip. Something about knowing we were leaving the mountain and heading for home today got my juices flowing.

"I'll wash the dishes after breakfast," I announced to my dad and Steve.

"Very unselfish of you, Johnny," my dad replied.

Actually, it was a pretty selfish move on my part. I wanted to do the dishes so I could get them done as fast as possible. Any delays meant more time in the mountains so I was willing to do whatever it took to get us out of there.

We only ate cold cereal that morning, which was great. No extra time spent trying to get water to boil or something to cook in a pan. It also meant less dishes to wash, so I finished them off quickly. I'm pretty sure I did a poor job of cleaning things because I was in such a hurry, but we wouldn't need them again on the trip anyway. Unless something crazy happened and we got stuck in the forest an extra day or so.

"No, that can't happen!" I blurted out by accident.

"What can't happen," my dad asked?

"Um, we can't, um, we can't (think, Johnny think), we

can't leave this spot without taking a selfie," I said, not knowing what I was saying. "I mean, it's our last campsite and I'll need a picture of it for the journal of our trip I'll be putting together when we get home."

Journal? What was I saying? The last thing I wanted was a reminder of any of this trip!

"Great idea, Johnny," my dad said. "We can all work on it together back home."

"Great." My brother said giving me an ugly stare. I think working on the journal was way down on his list also.

"Let's stand next to each other over here by these trees and rocks and capture this moment for all eternity."

Man, in trying not to have any delays I had caused another delay and what was worse, we were going to making a journal of our trip. I need to remember to keep my thoughts to myself from now on. It was time to just look straight ahead at the trail and walk!

My pack felt lighter, my legs felt stronger and my attitude felt much better. All because of knowing the clock was winding down on my first, and only, if I had anything to say about it, back-packing experience.

As we walked along the trail I eventually could see signs of civilization off in the distance and overtop of the trees.

"I'm saved!" I thought to myself. "I'm actually going to make it out of this forest alive."

After hiking for about an hour we came up on the river again. It seemed to be winding down the mountain much like we were. It was also picking up momentum much like we were. My walking pace had quickened and there were even times I took the lead on the hike and urged my dad and brother to keep up.

"Let's stop here for a quick break," my dad said.

"Okay, quick it is," I said. Then I set my watch alarm for two minutes and when the alarm sounded I popped up and said, "Let's go!"

"Not too fast," my dad said. "If we get to the parking lot at the bottom before your mom arrives with the car we're just going to have to sit there and wait for her. Besides, there a lot of good shots we could take here of the river and the rocks and trees for our journal."

This journal-thing was going to haunt me for weeks to come.

My dad waved us over so we could be in some of the pictures of the rocks and trees and rocks and trees. I know he was trying to kill some time so we didn't have to be stuck in the parking lot with nothing to do for too long, but he had no idea how great that sounded to me. Sitting in a parking lot, on flat ground, back in civilization with no more hiking or switchbacks sounded awesome. My brother, on the other hand, was still enjoying the wilderness and walked at his own pace, much slower than I liked for the next hour. I think he knew how much I wanted to be done with backpacking so he walked slower than normal just to torment me. It was typical older brother stuff, but I let it slide because the nightmare was almost over.

"Everybody stop. I want to take a picture of this pretty yellow flower," Steve said looking at me with a clever smirk on his face.

"Pretty yellow flower?" I thought. I don't think those words had ever come out of his mouth in his life, and probably never again. If there was anyone I knew that couldn't care less about flowers and if they were pretty, or yellow, it was my brother.

"I know what you're doing, Steve," I whispered to him with anger in my voice. "You're just slowing things down to bug me!"

"Speaking of bugs," he said. "Look at this interesting one over here. We need to take a few pictures of this guy."

"Stop it! I know you're just doing this to mess with my head." I said quietly but sternly.

"And, is it working?" He asked.

"Yes," I said.

"Good. Mission accomplished," he said with a laugh and then called my dad over to see the bug.

I decided at that point I would walk at my own pace for the rest of the trip and, if he decided just to stroll down the mountain instead, we would just leave him behind. Nothing was going to delay my escape from this mountain anymore!

Whoops! I spoke too soon.

My dad told us that around the next bend we might be able to see the edge of the parking lot a few hundred feet ahead. A few hundred feet sounded like nothing. I might even sprint the rest of the way!

"Only one small problem," my dad said.

Talk about a phrase you hate hearing. Have you ever had anyone say that phrase, *Only one small problem,* and had it actually be just a small problem? My heart began to sink as I thought of what the small problem might be.

I pictured my dad saying, "We'll be able to see the parking lot, but there's a small army waiting to shoot us down if we try to leave the forest!" Or, "There are man-eating trolls that guard the path and don't let anyone pass."

I didn't want to ask my dad what the "small problem" was. I just wanted to walk around that corner and see that the problem wasn't really much of a problem at all. Maybe the path was a little more narrow than usual and we'd have to be careful, and watch our step. Maybe there was a girl scout there and we couldn't leave the mountain without buying a box of cookies from her first.

"Please, for once, actually be something small!"

I needed the answer and didn't want the answer to the small problem, all at the same time. I just wanted to be out of this wilderness, now! Why couldn't things just be easy for once? Why did there have to be a problem at all, big or small?

"Why are you always testing me like this, God?" I asked under my breath. "Why do you always throw in difficult stuff when you could just make things easy on me? Are you doing it because you think it will make me a better person? Do you think I'll understand life and be able to handle it more? Because all you've done on this trip is make me upset with my dad for planning it, mad at my brother for doing big-brother stuff the whole time, and made me not very excited about the mountains! If that was your plan all along, well, then it worked."

My rant with God went on for a few minutes longer until I realized I wasn't going to win the argument or be able to change the outcome of my situation. He was God and I was me. It was no match. In the midst of my pity-party I remembered a verse from the Bible I had heard at church that said *God works all things for the good for those who loved Him,* and I knew I did love Him, in some way. I mean, He did send his only Son, Jesus, down here to die for me. That was some serious love!

When I thought about the sacrifice God made to send Jesus and what Jesus went through on this earth just so I could be with

Him in Heaven one day made this small trouble awaiting us around the corner start to shrink in comparison. In fact, all my complaints about this trip began to grow smaller and smaller as I thought of Jesus and his last days here on earth. Jesus had to climb a hill, too. With an incredible weight on his back and legs and body aching but He just kept going – for you and me.

"Okay, God. Messaged received." I said softly. I can take whatever the world dishes out because I know you'll be there with me to help me fight through it – even switchbacks!

I didn't need to ask my dad what the small problem might be awaiting us. One, because I was now ready to take it on, and two, because as we rounded the bend I recognized what the problem was right away - and it was *not* a small one.

Yes, we could see the path that led to the parking lot like my dad had said, but he failed to mention that standing between us and that path to the parking lot was the creek we had been encountering throughout our journey. Only, at this point, it was no longer a little creek. It was a mighty rushing river wider and stronger than all the times we ran into it while hiking! The sound of the rushing water was loud and I really had to focus on what my dad was saying to hear him and he was only a few feet away. He motioned Steve and I to follow him up river a bit where the river seemed a bit quieter but not any less fierce. This river meant business and you could tell just by looking at it that if you foolishly attempted to cross it, it would sweep you away and carry you downstream forever - if you didn't drown first. How were we going to get home?

The three of us just stood at the bank of the mighty river and stared at its fury. Even my always in control brother, Steve, appeared to be unnerved thinking we might have to try and cross this beast to get out of here.

"This is the small problem, dad?!" I shouted over the sound of the rushing water.

"Okay, it's bigger than the backpacking brochure mentioned," he said, trying to sound confident. "The snow this winter must have been bigger than in years past and there is a touch more water from the snow melting than normal."

"A touch more? There's a whole ocean more!" I shouted.

"What are we going to do, dad?" My brother asked.

"Become mountain men for the rest of our lives," I thought to myself. "We're going to have to hunt animals for food and make our clothes out of their skins."

I wondered if bearskin pants rubbed your legs as bad as jeans did when they got wet.

"With my luck, probably," I thought.

"We have two choices," my dad said as he pointed to our left, down river. "We can walk about ten miles that way where the map says there might be a bridge that crosses over the river, and then walk the ten miles back here to the trail. Or, we can cross the river over there where that log has fallen across the river, and be out of here in no time."

Did my dad just say what I thought he said? Maybe I wasn't hearing him right due to the noise of the river.

"Dad, it almost sounded like you said crossing the river was our best option."

"Yes, Johnny. We can walk across that log over there and be out of here in fifteen minutes at the most.

"That's great, dad," I said. "Except for one thing - *THERE'S NO WAY I'M CROSSING THIS RIVER ON A LOG!*"

I prayed my dad was joking. You know, one of those back-packing in the mountain jokes that all backpackers tell each other when they get together. That's all this was. Just a little joke.

"Very funny, dad," I said. "You still have your sense of humor, I see."

'It's not a joke, Johnny," my brother said with anger in his voice. "These are the only two options and you just need to face it. Besides, walking across that log will be easy so don't wimp out like you always do and we'll all be fine! If you chicken out it just means we all stay here longer than we need to. Or, even worse, dad might decide to have us make the twenty mile hike because you can't handle a simple log, which is NOT an option for me!"

Wow. I had seen my brother mad before, but this was one of his maddest! He looked like a bull that had seen enough of the red cape in a bullfight and had decided to go straight for the mata-dor! I don't think he'd throw me in the river and be done with me but he sure looked like he wanted to. I needed to get a hold of myself before he got a hold of me and tossed me in!

I looked over to the right at the log my dad was referring to and then to the left at the ten-plus-ten equals twenty mile hike that "might" have a bridge and neither of these options were working for me.

"For the last time, are you kidding us dad?" I shouted. I was hoping in a big way he was, but deep down I knew he wasn't.

"I'm not kidding, Johnny. We have two options and that's it," he said.

Well then, just call me *Jungle Johnny* from now on because I'm going to be living out the rest of my childhood here in the wilderness, or, at least until I develop the ability to jump twenty feet and clear this river in a single bound.

84

"Let's go check out the log," my dad said.

"Let's not," I thought.

My brother, on the other hand, ran towards the log with a kind of excitement. He even jumped up on the end of the log and looked across with a glow on his face. He probably loved the idea of such an adventure. A death- defying walk over a rushing river on a questionable log was right up his alley. Who is this guy? There was no way this was my real brother. We were so different when it came to things like this - and most everything else. We couldn't possibly have the same mother and father. Maybe he was adopted and my parents never told us. Maybe he's the son of that Bear Grylls guy from that Man vs. Wild show on TV and Bear couldn't live in the Amazon, or wherever in the world they dropped him, and have to take a baby along with him. I just stared at him as he jumped up and down on the log a bit to test its strength. I could tell he wanted to race across it right then. Even ahead of my dad! He looked like a kid in the Disneyland parking lot who couldn't wait for the doors to open so he could run to the Pirates of the Caribbean ride and be the first one on the boat.

"Yeah, he's definitely not my real brother," I decided.

"Easy, Steve," my dad said. "Let me check it out first. If I don't think it is safe then we won't be crossing it."

"Don't be safe! Don't be safe!" I kept repeating under my breath.

My brother jumped down, reluctantly, and my dad climbed up. He bounced a bit to check its strength much like my brother did. He took a few steps to see if it would balance him without shifting or moving. He spent a good amount of time checking every possible scenario possible and when he was done he turned to us and said, "We can do this."

85

My cry of despair was drowned out by brothers giant, "Woohoo!"

"Woohoo! We're all going to die!" I figured.

My dad made us all get up on the end of the log so we could watch him walk across. He wanted us to see exactly where he stepped and how. I stayed as far back and away from the river as possible. I wasn't going near the edge if I didn't have to. Of course, my brother was right up on the edge and looking down at the river taunting it.

"Come and get me, little river." Steve said with a laugh.

"Step back, Steve," my dad said. "I'm going across. Watch my steps carefully and try to remember where my feet land on the log. As long as the log feels sturdy and stays in place, I'll keep going. If I think for one moment that it's not safe I'll turn around and come back, right away."

"Johnny, can you see my steps from back there?" my dad asked.

"I'm good. I can see all I need to see from here," I said with panic in my voice. "I love you, dad." I figured I'd better get that in in case I never saw him again."

"I love you, too," he said. "This will be easy, trust me."

And, with that, he turned towards the river, looked down at the log and took the first step. Everything seemed okay, so he took another then another, one cautious step at a time. He continued, step by step, moving towards the other side of the river gaining confidence with each step. Secretly, I was hoping the log would fail the test and my dad would turn around and come back. If he made it across he would make us do the same. Of course, my brother had other ideas and was cheering him on.

When dad reached the other side safely he turned and

looked at us with a big smile on his face.

"Pretty easy," he hollered back at us. "Stay in the middle, watch where you step, stop when you need to regain your balance and you'll make it. It's about as wide as the sidewalk at home. You can walk on that without falling off of it, right?"

"Most of the time," I thought to myself.

Having the reassurance of my dad, my brother began to walk across the log. He was moving quickly, faster than my dad had done it. Everything was a challenge to him. That's probably why he was so great at things.

"Slow down, Steve," my dad said. "It's not a race."

Are you kidding? Of course to Steve it was a race. When he reached the other side without a problem he jumped up and down like he had just won the decathlon at the Olympics, or stuck the landing on the parallel bars.

Either way, you would have thought my confidence would have improved because of how easy it seemed for Steve, but it hadn't. I was now even more nervous than before because my brother and my dad were safely on one side of the river and I was alone on the, *I'm going to be living in the wilderness forever,* side.

"Piece of cake, just like I said, Johnny!" My brother shouted to me as he waved at me to come across.

My dad climbed back out onto the log and moved to the edge of the river on his side. He motioned for me to do the same on my side of the log.

"Get near the edge, Johnny and I'll talk you through this!" he shouted. "You'll be fine and we'll all be home in a couple hours!"

What else could I do with them on one side of this massive river and me on the other? So, I crept out, sheepishly, on the log towards the edge of the river, then stepped back quickly. The sound of the river when I neared the edge was so powerful it startled me. I knew at that moment, in my heart, I couldn't do this.

"Dad, it's been nice knowing you!" I shouted, knowing I would probably never see him again. "Steve, well, let me think about it."

Chapter 8 Word Study & Doodle on Pages 128-129

# CHAPTER NINE
## "FATHER TO THE RESCUE!"

Standing on that fallen log, shaking with fear as I watched the violent river rushing under it and seeing my dad and brother safety on the other side had me convinced I'd never see either of them again. In my mind I took back the thought that if I never saw my brother again I might not miss him. I knew, deep down, I would miss my brother in a big way if I never saw him again. But brothers don't say that kind of stuff to each other, do they?

"Maybe they should," I thought.

I knew I was going to have to call on him time and time again to make it through the rest of my life and I knew he'd always be there if I called. He liked being the protective big brother.

Hey, maybe he would have to call on me for help when we got older. I would be that successful billionaire brother, like you see in the movies, and he would be my adventurous brother whose good looks and serious skill set only got him so far in life and he needed someone to bail him out of trouble. I'd tell him I couldn't help him, at first. That he needed to get himself back on his own two feet. I'd give him the speech that I had to scratch and claw my way to the top and he would have to also. I'd remind him that life is hard and you have to work for everything you get.

Then he'd smile and remind me how he saved my life when we were kids by helping me cross that enormous river on our backpacking adventure. We'd laugh about it and then I'd hand him a few thousand dollars and tell him to take care of himself. He'd smile, hug me and then disappear for a few months. Good times.

"Johnny, you can do this! I promise!" My dad shouted taking me away from my penthouse offices in some big Metropolis and landing me right back on this log.

"Step out a bit further on the log closer to where the river edge is – but when you get there, don't look down!"

"Don't look down?" I gasped. "Don't say that!"

What do you do when someone tells you not to look down? You look down, don't you? It's like there is this muscle in the back of your neck that waits until it hears that phrase and then automatically grabs your head and forces you to look down.

So, instinctively, or because of that stinking muscle in my neck, what did I do? I looked down – and, man, was sorry I did!

I realized, instantly, why my dad didn't want me to look down at the river because the current was so swift and powerful it was unnerving. It looked like a runaway train racing down its tracks at top speed and out of control! It was rushing so fast to the left that it actually tricked my eyes into thinking the log was actually moving to the right. It was an optical illusion, I knew it, but it looked so real. I was going to have a hard enough time trying to cross a log that was stationary, but a moving one – no way!

"Dad!" I screamed. "The log is moving to the right!"

"No it's not, son! It just looks like it is!" He said, thinking that would comfort me, which it didn't.

"What's the difference?!" I hollered back. "You want me to

92

cross over this rushing river on a log that appears to be moving to the right?"

"Don't focus on the river," he said. "Focus on the log and picture every place I stepped. Put your feet where you feel I did. Step in my steps and you'll make it across, just like your brother did."

I looked over at my brother and he was actually encouraging me.

"You can do this, Johnny! I believe in you!"

"Wow! He's never said anything like that to me before. A guy will say anything for a few thousand bucks," I thought.

Then my dad spoke up again and caught me off guard by what he said.

"Oh, and Johnny, before you start, I need you to undo the belt on your backpack."

"Why?" I fired back.

"Don't ask why, just do it," he said.

"Okay," I said. Then I instinctively asked, "Why?" one more time. I had to know. I just had to know. I probably didn't want to know but I had to know.

My dad finally realized I wasn't going to stop asking.

"Well," he said hesitantly, "in case you might happen to step wrong, *which is not going to happen!* But, if for some reason the unthinkable was to happen and you were to stumble a bit and fall off the log, *which is not going to happen!*" He continued. "You don't want to be attached to your backpack because it could drag you under the water and take you downstream without you being able to fight it or stop yourself...*which is not going to happen!*"

"Why did I have to ask why?"

Now I was less confident than ever, but I had my belt undone in a matter of seconds. You don't have to tell me twice about being dragged down by the river and never heard from again, *which is not going to happen*, according to my dad.

"Look directly at me," my dad said, "and take a couple of steps."

I tried to muster up every bit of courage I could and then took one step further out on the log.

"That's one small step for man - One giant leap for scardy-cats everywhere!"

I could now hear the rushing water underneath me more than ever. The log was shaking from the force of the water pounding against the bank of the river beneath me. I was scared and I'm sure my dad and brother could see the panic on my face!

"Focus on me, Johnny," he urged. "It's just you and me here, nothing else. Take it one step at a time!"

I did my best to block out everything around me and just focus on my dad. It was hard with the noise, the spray from the river and my brother pointing at me and making weight-lifter poses. This was no time to be trying to make me laugh. My life was on the line, but, obviously, Steve didn't see the magnitude of my fear.

I kept listening to my dad's encouragement and kept creeping forward, step by step. Soon, I realized, somehow, I had made it halfway across the log. That was great and *not great* all at the same time. It felt like I was in no man's land. Still a long way from my dad but now too far to go back where I had started. So I froze.

The helpless feeling of standing alone over the violent water and trying to figure out what I was even doing out here, actually reminded me of a story from the Bible I had heard in our Youth Group a few weeks earlier.

It was the story in the Book of Matthew of when Jesus walked on the water, and Peter, one of his apostles decided he wanted to join him.

When Jesus asked Peter to be one of the twelve apostles, Peter seemed to take charge right from the beginning. He was a leader-type, so if you put him with a group of men he would most likely take over and do whatever he could to lead the others and set a good example. He failed many times, but Jesus always forgave him and actually called him the Rock Jesus could build his church on someday. So, you can imagine, when confronted with a scary situation, Peter would most likely be the one to step up and handle it - like he did in this great Bible story.

In the story in Matthew, Jesus had spent most of the day miraculously feeding thousands of people. He and his disciples were tired and Jesus asked them to get into a boat and sail to the other side of the nearby lake on their own and he would join them later once he was done saying good-bye to the crowd.

Later that night, with their boat far from shore and being blown hard by the wind and tossed by the waves, Jesus appeared to them walking on the water about a hundred feet from their boat. The first person to look out on the water and see someone walking on it freaked out! Wouldn't you? There was a man walking on water! You didn't see that every day. In fact, no one had ever seen anything like it, ever! Soon they were all freaking out!

"It's a ghost!" One of them shouted, and they all ducked down out of fear, but not Peter. He just stared out at the mystery man.

"Don't be afraid!" The man on the water shouted to them. "It's only me, Jesus!"

The shouting and screaming on the boat went silent as they

all looked up and stared out at the man they had just spent the day with. They couldn't believe their eyes.

Then the silence broke.

"If that really is you, Jesus," a voice called from the group, "have me walk out to you!" The voice, of course, was Peter's.

I can imagine the other disciples looking over at Peter with thoughts of disbelief.

"Are you kidding?" Some of them shouted.

"Peter, did you hear what you just said?" One of the disciples might have asked. "I think you ate too much fish today!"

Peter had always been the most daring and most outspoken of them all, but this was a ridiculous request, even for Peter. Ridiculous to everyone, that is, except Jesus who responded to Peter's request.

"Come on out, Peter!"

"What?" They all thought to themselves. "Is Jesus trying to drown Peter?" It was night and they were far from shore on a stormy sea. Everyone who knew the sea, especially Peter, a fisherman, knew the safest place to be in a situation like this was on a sturdy boat. They all looked at Peter waiting for him to call out to Jesus and tell him he was just kidding, but instead, Peter reached for the rail of the boat and lifted his leg as if to climb out.

I can picture one of the disciples saying, "Okay, Peter, fun time is over! Now get back in this boat! You've reminded us again that you're the brave one but this is no joke, get back in this boat!"

But, Peter turned a deaf ear to their urging and reached his foot down towards the swirling ocean. Still holding onto the boat, he touched his foot down on the surface of the water and it felt wet but it also felt firm – his foot did not sink! Can you see the other disciples in the boat looking over the edge and staring down at

Peter's foot only to see it resting on the top of the water as if it was on solid ground?

"Whoa!" They probably said to each other in amazement.

Then Peter continued and set his other foot down on the water and it rested on the surface also. He might still be holding onto the edge of the boat but looked up at the disciples as if to say, "Check this out!"

I imagine some of the disciples were in awe of the situation and told Peter to go for it, to walk towards Jesus, and maybe there were other voices questioning and even urging Peter more to get back in the boat.

But, Peter blocked everything out, turned his head towards Jesus and only heard one voice, the voice of Jesus saying, "Come on Peter!"

Keeping his head turned and his eyes on Jesus, I picture Peter taking one hand off the boat and then slowly the other and not sinking.

"Whoa! Again they all shouted as they stared at Peter miraculously being held up only by the power of the man who was calling him towards him, Jesus.

Peter did everything he could to not show fear as he turned his back completely on the boat and focused only on Jesus who was urging Peter to move towards him and away from the boat. It was if Jesus was telling him, "Move away from your old life, Peter, and walk my direction. Let go of your old life and what you think will keep you safe and trust me instead."

With each step Peter gained more and more confidence as he moved closer to Jesus and further from the boat. He kept his eyes on Jesus and was doing the unthinkable, walking on water! Everything was going well, too, until the wind whipped a bigger wave than the others the storm had been stirring up and it caught Peter by surprise. For a quick instant Peter took his eyes off of Jesus and as the Bible tells it, he began to sink.

Realizing his life was in jeopardy; Peter quickly looked back at Jesus and did the best thing he could have ever done. He cried out, "Help me, Jesus! Help me!"

Jesus gladly reached out his hand and took a hold of Peter's, pulled him up and out of the water and led him back to the boat. Jesus and Peter climbed into the boat, and I imagine everyone just stared at them. The Bible says at that moment that Jesus wasn't just an ordinary man but truly the Son of God.

A great reminder to trust Jesus in all your journeys and call on Him in times of trouble.

I can remember when we studied this story in our youth group I told myself if I had been out on that rough sea I wouldn't have let the ocean waves distract me. I would stay more focused on Jesus than Peter did.

Well, I was about to find out if that was true or not.

"Johnny!" My dad called out.

The sound of his voice, and the violent sound of the ocean, I mean river, below snapped me out of my daydream.

I woke to realize, unfortunately, I was still at the halfway point on the log and still scared but glad I hadn't fallen off during my temporary loss of focus. I looked over at my dad who was, much like Jesus on the ocean, encouraging me to keep my eyes on him and continue to move in his direction. He even stepped out a bit further on the log and stretched out his hand towards me making him appear even closer to me than before. I continued to focus on him with each careful step and was starting to think I might actually be able to do this. I might actually make it across safely. I was just a couple of steps away from his hand and feeling good.

Just then, in the midst of so much good, everything went horribly bad! A branch that had broken away from a tree upstream came rushing down the river and smacked into the log I was standing on. The jolt from the two logs colliding unnerved me and caused me to stumble a bit. In a panic, I took my eyes off of my dad for just a few seconds to see what had caused the loud noise and shook the log. In that brief instance, I started to lose my balance and felt myself starting to slip off of the log.

"Why did logs have to be round?" I asked myself. "Why couldn't they be flat like the ground?"

There was no time for an answer. Round or flat I was falling off! I quickly looked back at my dad and, much like Peter did when he knew he was in trouble, I cried out to him.

"Dad, help me!"

Out of the corner of my eye I saw my brother throw off his pack, jump down off the log and run to the bank down river. He was ready to jump in after me if I fell off the log. Can you believe that?

Side Note: If you have a big brother or big sister like that go give them a hug! Do it right now if they're around. Even if they don't know what it's for and push you away and tell you to leave them alone, hug them anyway. This adventure will be here when you get back!

I looked back from my brother to my dad who, by this time, had moved as far out on the log as he could without coming out and making it hard for two of us to make it off safely. He reached out his hand as far as he could; stretching every muscle in his body as far as possible.

"Grab my hand, Johnny!" He shouted as he stretched.

I reached my hand towards his hoping I could grab it before I lost my balance completely and tumbled off the log and into the rushing river. My dad's face looked determined and it gave me confidence.

"One finger," I thought. "If I can just get a hold of one finger I'm sure that will be enough!"

His hand was close, very close! But was it close enough?

Chapter 9 Word Study & Doodle on Pages 130-131

# CHAPTER TEN
## "BACKPACK FOR SALE!"

I knew all was lost. I wasn't going to make it! I wasn't going to be able to grab my dad's hand in time to keep from plunging into the violent river below! I was sure I was seconds away from falling into the river, never to be seen again. But my dad wasn't giving up so easily. He made one last lunge for me stretching his body beyond what looked possible and, miraculously, caught hold of my hand at the last second. He held on with all of his might! I felt strength in his grip I never knew he had! With one huge heave he stood me back up on the log and I was able to get my footing again. I eagerly followed my dad and took the last few steps to the end of the log. I had made it! I had made it all the way across! Over the rushing river! Out of the wilderness and I was still alive!

I instantly hugged my dad and didn't let go. I couldn't stop thanking him for saving me. He told me I had done most of the work myself but I knew that wasn't true. I knew inside he had saved me.

"I never should have taken my eyes off of you, dad," I said while still hugging him. "I should have stayed focused!"

"That's easy to say now, Johnny," he said. "But when

103

you're in the moment it's a lot harder, isn't it?"

"It sure was," I thought to myself.

I guess I would have messed up just as bad as or even worse than Peter, if I had been on that boat when Jesus appeared. I made a mental note to find Peter when I got to heaven and apologize for thinking I could have done it better.

Once I was done hugging my dad and getting a rare high-five from my brother, I turned and just stared at the log and the river. I still couldn't quite believe I had made it across. Just minutes earlier I knew for a fact I couldn't have done this, but with the confidence my dad had in me, a lot of focusing and just enough courage, I had done the unthinkable. I had, kind of, walked on water. It was a *mountain miracle* I would remember for the rest of my life.

I would never forget this day and the life-lesson it taught me. I needed to keep my eyes on Jesus no matter how stormy my life would get. No matter what craziness happened around me, I needed to remember to always focus on Him in times of trouble and He would help me get through them.

My dad suggested we sit on the bank for a few minutes before we headed out to the parking lot and thank God for everything we had experienced on our backpacking adventure. As much as I wanted to be out of the forest and safely in the parking lot which was only a few hundred feet away, I also wanted to take time to thank God myself as well.

We took off our backpacks and sat next to each other on the bank of the river and just looked out. No one said anything for awhile, we just stared and watched the water rush by. I prayed silently and thanked God for everything I had experienced, good and bad, on this trip. I learned a lot about me. I also saw some amazing sights, some incredible sunsets, a giant moon and almost got washed away by a river. Good times!

I also knew my relationship with my dad, and even my brother, grew that weekend. And, I felt closer to Jesus than I ever had before in my life, too. Peter became an amazing follower of Jesus and many people today are close to Jesus because of Peter's trust in Him. Count me as one of them.

We stayed on the bank of the river for about ten minutes and then my dad got up and we joined him. He put his pack on and said, "Let's go home."

"Amen to that!" I said, grabbing my pack and putting it on for what I figured was the last time ever in my life. Sure, I learned a lot on this weekend and this was an incredible adventure, but I was pretty sure I would never, ever want to go through it all again. My legs were tired and still had sores on them from walking in wet jeans. My back still ached, my neck ached, my shoulders ached! Let's face it, my whole body ached. I couldn't wait to eat real food and sleep in a real bed with a pillow that was actually soft. Back-packing might be for some people, but I wasn't one of them.

We walked down the path towards the parking lot and as we got closer the sound of the river behind us grew quieter and quieter until I couldn't hear it anymore. Our wilderness adventure was over and I couldn't wait to tell my mom, Henry, Richie and especially Summer about all I had experienced.

I'm sure my mom would be glad I was still alive. Henry and Richie would probably make me tell them all the details about almost falling off the log and almost dying over and over again.

Summer, hopefully, would be glad I was still alive also and, of course, she would be excited my relationship with Jesus had grown closer.

"Mom!" I yelled, spotting her next to the car as we reached the parking lot. I ran to her and gave her a big hug almost knocking her over. I forgot I still had my backpack on. She hugged me back and gave my brother a big hug when he walked up also. He gave her a small hug back.

"C'mon, mom," Steve said, pulling away from my mom's grasp. "We were only gone three days."

Steve had reached that age where he thought hugging your mom in public was questionable, but not me. Besides, we were the only people in the parking lot so I could make a fool of myself and no one would notice. Besides, seeing her meant we'd be in the car and home soon.

My dad walked up, took off his pack and gave my mom a big hug and kiss.

"How did it go?" she asked my dad. "How did my moun-taineers do?"

"Great!" my dad said, looking over at my brother and me. "Everything went smoothly. No real incidents to speak of, right boys?"

"No incidents?" I thought to myself. "Except for zillions of switchbacks, me falling in a creek, having to walk for miles in wet jeans, eating gross food, a sarcastic trout and almost washing away in a giant river never to be seen again - only all that!"

I know what my dad was doing. If we shared all the possible danger we faced, my mom might say no to any adventures in the future, so it would be better to keep certain details about the

106

trip to ourselves, at least for now, anyway. We both just nodded our heads in agreement with my dad.

We piled our backpacks in the car, climbed in and drove for home. We did share all the great things we had experienced with my mom as we drove. She liked hearing about the amazing sunsets and giant moon. She laughed as I told her about the Tommy the trout. We told story after story which made the drive home go by fast. We were off the freeway and in our town in no time. My mom asked if anyone was hungry for a burger and fries. Three huge "Yeses" echoed in the car.

My mom turned into our favorite burger place in town, "World Burger," and pulled up to the drive in. The smell of burgers and French fries was amazing! I couldn't wait to bite into a double cheese burger! No, make it a double World Burger, the biggest burger on their menu! I was that hungry!

"Anybody want chili on their burger?" My mom asked.

"No chili!" All three of us shouted at the same time and then we all laughed together. My mom wondered what was so funny about asking us if we wanted chili and my dad told her about our attempted chili cooking adventure and we laughed as we ate in the car for the rest of the ride home.

Dad shared a few more of our fun experiences with my mom until we got home. No near-death or life-in-peril stuff though. Maybe years from now it might be okay to tell the whole story to her, but not now.

When we got home I was so relieved to step out of the car and onto the familiar, and flat, ground of our street. I stretched and gave a loud stretching sigh of relief.

"Home, sweet, home," I said as I stretched, which was followed by an unexpected giggle from behind me. I turned around to see where the giggle was coming from and there was Summer, next door, sitting on her front lawn. She gave me a wave and a smile. Have I mentioned that smile?

"Had she been sitting there the whole time waiting for me to return?" I wondered, which I instantly followed with, "Dream on!"

"I'll be in, in a minute," I said. "I'm going over to say hi to Summer."

"Don't snuggle up too close," my brother said with a laugh. "You smell pretty bad - even worse than normal."

"Ha! Ha!" I said, though he was probably right. I hadn't showered for three days and was just coming back from being in the wilderness for days. I took a quick whiff of my armpit without her noticing as I walked up. Yikes, my pits were nasty! I smelled like a can of tuna that got left in the sun for days. I probably looked like a can of tuna that had been left in the sun for days also. I kept a safe distance from her as I approached.

"How was your backpacking trip, Johnny?" She asked.

"It was cool!" I said, sitting down about three feet from her. I hoped that was enough distance to keep her from smelling the stench coming off of me.

"Did anything interesting happen?" She asked, almost as if she knew something did. I knew she and God were close, but I didn't know they talked about me on a regular basis.

"Well, I did almost drown," I said as calmly as I could. I wanted her to think I could face death and just laugh about it. I figured it would make me look manlier to her. Why was I so concerned about looking or seeming manlier to her? What was it about Summer that made me always want to brag or appear to be more than I really was?

"What do you mean, you almost drowned?" She asked with concern.

I went on to tell her about our entire backpacking adventure. I shared everything. Falling in the creek, wet jeans, nasty Mac and Cheese, gooey chili, the sunsets, the moon and almost falling off the log and how my dad rescued me. I even told her stuff I promised myself I would never share with anyone. About how scared I was at certain times. How much the hiking hurt all over. How much I complained. How much of a sissy I was. I couldn't believe how honest I was being with her about my feelings. I even told her how my relationship with Jesus had grown on this trip. I told her things I would never share with Henry or Richie, or anyone. Not even my mom and dad.

"Who was this girl who lived next door to me?" I asked myself. "Why do I want to tell her everything – the good, the bad and the ugly?"

"Sounds like you had a great time. I imagine you can't wait until you get to go backpacking again," she said.

"Oh, no!" I said. "Once was good enough for me! I'm never going backpacking again!"

"Never say never, Johnny. God might have other plans in mind."

"Not even God could come up with a plan great enough to put me back in those mountains again!" I said with confidence.

"What if, in a few years from now a group of my girl friends and I wanted to go backpacking, and we needed a few strong men to go along to keep us safe?" She asked. "Should I ask Henry and Richie to go along instead of you?"

"No, I mean, yes. I mean, of course not! I mean, I think I'd go, I mean…," I was stumbling with my words like a boxer who had just taken a hard punch to the head. I needed to say something better, and quickly. Something that let her know I would be there for her whenever she needed me.

But, of course, as luck would have it, as I struggled to find the right words to say, Henry and Richie rounded the corner of my street on bikes and headed our way. I wanted to give Summer a better answer to her question but I couldn't now. Not with these two jokers approaching.

"We can pick up this conversation later, Johnny," Summer said as she got up and headed for her front door.

"Don't leave on our account," Henry said as he rode up. "You two can still work on your wedding plans together if you want. We don't mind." Then he and Richie both laughed.

"Be quiet you guys!" I shouted at them. "Sorry, Summer."

She just smiled like it was no problem. Nothing ever seemed to bother her.

"Isn't she twelve like the rest of us," I asked myself? "Who is this girl who lives next door to me?"

"Whoa, you smell rank!" Richie said. "You need a shower bad!"

"Oh, man!" I thought. "He was five feet away from me and could smell me and I'd just spent fifteen minutes sitting three feet away from Summer. How embarrassing!"

"I think he smells manly," Summer said as she opened the front door of her house. "Remember, Johnny, you owe me a better answer later," she said. Then she winked at me and went her house and closed the door.

"A better answer?" Henry questioned. "I knew it! Summer *has* asked you to marry her!" He said with a giant laugh. Richie joined in the laughter - but I didn't. These two were so immature

110

when it came to girls. All I could do was let them laugh it out, and then I could down to the serious business of telling them about my amazing backpacking adventure.

I spent a good hour sharing the entire adventure with them and they hit me with question after question until it started to get dark. I forgot how sore and tired I was, I just kept talking.

"Wow, Johnny, What an awesome adventure, Henry said. "I'm going home right now and tell my dad we need to go back-packing!"

"Me too!" Richie shouted.

"You too? Why are you going to my house to tell my dad you need to go backpacking?" Henry said, thinking he was clever.

"Ha! Ha!" Richie said. "You know what I meant!" Then we all broke out laughing again!

"Maybe we could all go together," Richie said.

"Yeah! That would be awesome!" Henry said. "The Three Amigos Attacking the Wilderness! What do you say, Johnny?"

"I say, I'm putting my backpack on the sidewalk tomorrow with a sign on it that says, 'BACKPACK FOR SALE.' I've had enough backpacking for a lifetime. I'll find other ways to get closer to God and nature and almost dying from now on."

"I totally understand," Henry said. "When something takes you that close to death you never want to be around it again. That's why you'll never catch me near Suicide Hill or Frog Finger ever again. Besides, you've got a wedding to plan, Johnny."

And, with that we all started laughing uncontrollably. I jumped on Henry, wrestled him to the ground, stuck my armpit in his face and said, "Marry this!"

The three of us wrestled for another ten minutes until we

111

couldn't breathe.

My dad came out carrying the three backpacks. He had emptied them out and wiped them down.

"Johnny, will you help me put these up in the rafters of the garage?" He asked.

I wanted to tell him to just leave them on the curb in hopes someone would drive by and grab them.

"Sure," I said while climbing off of Henry and Richie.

"I'll see you guys tomorrow," I said, heading for my house.

"I won't call you before noon, Johnny." Henry said. "It will take you that long to decontaminate from that nasty smell!"

Henry and Richie jumped on their bikes and rode off laughing.

I ran into the garage and my dad already had the ladder in place and was climbing it.

"Hand them to me one at a time and I'll put them on this high shelf and out of the way," my dad said.

I gave him his orange one and my brothers blue one. My dad reached way up high and put them both out of sight. I knew first-hand about my dad's incredible reach now. I then grabbed my green one and stared at it for a second before handing it to him.

"You don't look dorky green to me," I said as I lifted it up to my dad. He reached up and I watched as my backpack went out of sight.

"I wonder if we'll remember those are up there if we ever need them again," my dad questioned as he climbed down the stairs. "You know what they say, 'Out of sight, out of mind.'"

Out of sight, maybe, but never out of mind. What I learned on this *mountain miracle* would stay with me for the rest of my life. Hopefully, the nasty way I smelled wouldn't! - THE END!

Chapter 10 Word Study & Doodle on Pages 132-133

# Word Study &
# DOODLE PAGES

Along with a great message about "Trust" in this book, "Johnny Lazarus in Mountain Miracle," there are also many other great messages found in each chapter about how to live a godly life as well.

Take out a Bible and spend some time studying these cool words in each Word Study. They will help become the person God always intended you to be. Take some time to pray and ask God to help you place the true meaning of each word in your heart as you prepare for a new day.

Also, get your *creativity* on and doodle your best memory from each chapter as well on the Doodle Pages. Look back on them often and laugh and enjoy your masterpiece over and over again. Share them with your friends and family as well so you can all experience the Mountain Miracle Johnny did!

# Chapter 1
# "CREATION"

Dictionary definition: "The action or process of bringing something into existence."

In this first chapter, Johnny realizes he is going to see God's CREATION up close and personal when he and his brother go backpacking in the mountains with their dad. Remember Johnny's dad describing the adventure they are about to take?

*"This won't be an easy trip," my dad said. "But it will be rewarding and you'll get to see a part of God's creation that few people ever get to see. You'll remember this adventure forever."*

You will here in your lifetime many views of how people believe this world was created and mountains and rivers and even people were formed. But, the Bible (God's Word) reminds us that He is the creator all things as you can read in the Book of Genesis.

*Power Memory Verse* on the word **CREATION**.

*In the beginning God created the heavens and the earth. [2] Now the earth was formless and empty, darkness was over the surface of the deep, and the Spirit of God was hovering over the waters. – Genesis 1:1-2*

Read the rest of Genesis 1 if you have time and start your day reminded that God is in charge of all CREATION!

# CHAPTER 1 - DOODLE PAGE
## Draw Your Favorite Memory from Chapter 1

# Chapter 2
# "HUMILITY"

Dictionary definition: "A modest view of someone's importance; humbleness."

Having HUMILITY, or learning to be humble, is hard to do isn't it? We want people to brag about us when we do well, but sometimes we tend to brag for ourselves also. Johnny was always trying to do better than his brother, Steve, and the minute he thought he did he boasted about himself, remember this?

*My brother was still in his room with his door shut. He, too, was filling his backpack.*
*"At least I was faster than him at something," I thought.*
*When I got to the front of the house my mom and dad weren't around, so I decided to head out into the neighborhood on my own.*

Johnny congratulates himself for being faster than his brother. It's okay to feel good about yourself, but we need to remember to show HUMILITY when doing so. Our good deeds should make people praise God instead of ourselves, like it says in Matthew.

**Power Memory Verse** on the word **HUMILITY**.

*"… Let your light shine before others, that they may see your good deeds and praise your Father in Heaven." Matt. 5:16*

# CHAPTER 2 - DOODLE PAGE
## Draw Your Favorite Memory from Chapter 2

# Chapter 3
# "LISTENER"

Dictionary definition: "Someone who listens in an attentive manner."

Johnny's friendship with Summer Breeze was based largely on her ability to just listen to him. Johnny knew he could share his heart openly with her knowing her silence just might provide the right answers for him. Here's how Johnny described it.

*"Most of our time we spent together was just talking. She was a good talker and an even better listener."*

God is also a great listener. The Bible says we should pray to Him with all kinds of prayer knowing He hears us and will answer us. Listen to this verse in Psalm.

***Power Memory Verse*** on the word **LISTENER**.

***"The righteous cry out, and the LORD hears them; he delivers them from all their troubles." Psalm 34:17***

Spend some time praying and listening to God. He will provide the answers you need.

# CHAPTER 3 - DOODLE PAGE
## Draw Your Favorite Memory from Chapter 3

# Chapter 4
# "PRAYER"

Dictionary definition: "A request for help or expression of thanks to God."

Following up with being a listener, which I mentioned in the Chapter 3 Word Study, I wanted to remind you to be a talker with God also. We too often try to solve problems on our own without calling on God for help. Or we call on Him last after we've messed everything up, don't we. This verse in 1 Thessalonians reminds us how important PRAYER can be.

_**Power Memory Verse**_ on the word **PRAYER**.

*"Rejoice always, [17] pray continually, [18] give thanks in all circumstances; for this is God's will for you in Christ Jesus."*
*1 Thessalonians 5: 16-18*

Maybe write a quick list of some of things you're thankful for and some requests you like to talk to God about and add a PRAYER time to your day.

# CHAPTER 4 - DOODLE PAGE
## Draw Your Favorite Memory from Chapter 4

# Chapter 5
# "TRIALS"

Dictionary definition: "A test to assess someone's abilities and performance."

Johnny realized, early in the hike, that this backpacking adventure was going to be a TRIAL, and he wasn't sure he had what it would take to see it through. Remember here where he was ready to give up before he has even started climbing the mountain.

*"My legs were feeling the weight of my pack with every step and I grew tired quickly. I was struggling with every step and we hadn't even started going up yet. We were still just walking on the part of the trail that would take us closer to the base of the mountain."*

The good news is that though it was tough this TRIAL Johnny faced made his faith in God stronger and helped prepare him for life's challenges ahead of him. This verse says it all!

**Power Memory Verse** on the word **TRIALS**.

*"Consider it pure joy, my brothers and sisters, whenever you face trials of many kinds, [3] because you know that the testing of your faith produces perseverance." James 1: 2, 3*

Pray for God's help to get you through any trials you might face.

# CHAPTER 5 - DOODLE PAGE
## Draw Your Favorite Memory from Chapter 5

# Chapter 6
# "SELF-CONTROL"

Dictionary definition: "Ability to control ones emotions in difficult times."

SELF-CONTROL is something Johnny, and most of us, need to be working on all the time. Remaining calm in difficult situations can be hard, especially if you let things build up to a boiling point. Remember here where Johnny exploded?

*"Ahhhh!" I screamed. I couldn't hold it in anymore! I had to let it all out! All the anger and frustration! All the hurt and cold! All the - everything!*
*"What's wrong, Johnny?" My dad said.*
*"What's wrong?" I shouted. "What's right? I want to go home, now! This was a bad idea from the start!*

Learning to have self-control in the hardest of times will gain you the respect of those around you. You will also make smarter and more rational decisions and be showing people what it means to have a heart and mind like Jesus.

**_Power Memory Verse_** on the word **SELF-CONTROL**.

*[5] ... add to your faith goodness; and to goodness, knowledge; [6] and to knowledge, self-control; and to self-control, perseverance; and to perseverance, godliness; [7] and to godliness, mutual affection; and to mutual affection, love. - 2 Peter 1: 5-8*

# CHAPTER 6 - DOODLE PAGE
## Draw Your Favorite Memory from Chapter 6

# Chapter 7
# "FAIRNESS"

Dictionary definition: "Impartial and just treatment without favoritism or discrimination."

Being treated unfairly can really hurt at times, can't it? It makes us angry and want to lash out at others. Johnny's reaction to feeling like he was being treated unfairly by his brother brought out the worst in him...and all because of a fish.

*"What?!" I shouted. "He's going to catch my fish! No fair! No fair! How could you let him do that, dad! That is my fish! I'm supposed to win the contest this time, not Steve!"*

FAIRNESS in life can come to us when we remember to treat others with FAIRNESS also. Always try to do the good, honest, right and fair things and life will go much easier for you and you'll be blessing others at the same time!

**Power Memory Verse** on the word **FAIRNESS**.

**"The Lord is a shield to those whose walk is blameless, 8 for he guards the course of the just and protects the way of his faithful ones. 9 Then you will understand what is right and just and fair—every good path." – Proverbs 2: 7-9**

Pray for a just heart today and so FAIRNESS to everyone.

# CHAPTER 7 - DOODLE PAGE
## Draw Your Favorite Memory from Chapter 7

# Chapter 8
# "UNSELFISH"

Dictionary definition: "Willing to put the needs of others before your own."

Doesn't it always seem like our own needs or desires are more important than others? Why do we always think of our own best interests firsts? Johnny tried to shorten the entire backpacking trip for his dad and brother because of his longing to be home.

*"Very unselfish of you, Johnny," my dad replied.*
*Actually, it was a pretty selfish move on my part. I wanted to do the dishes so I could get them done as fast as possible. Any delays meant more time in the mountains so I was willing to do whatever it took to get us out of there.*

Putting others first is one of the foundations of being the best follower of Jesus you can be. Jesus set the ultimate example of being UNSELFISH by dying on the cross for us. We need to work on thinking of others first like He did.

*Power Memory Verse* on the word **UNSELFISH**.

*[3] Do nothing out of selfish ambition or vain conceit. Rather, in humility value others above yourselves, [4] not looking to your own interests but each of you to the interests of the others. – Philippians 2: 3-4*

# CHAPTER 8 - DOODLE PAGE
## Draw Your Favorite Memory from Chapter 8

# Chapter 9
# "ENCOURAGEMENT"

Dictionary definition: "The act of giving someone support, confidence and hope."

Throughout my life I can remember conquering many challenges just because of someone encouraging me along the way. Johnny might have felt like he could never cross that rushing river, but ENCOURAGEMENT came from an unlikely source, his brother, Steve, and he made it across, remember?

> *"I looked over at my brother and he was actually encouraging me.*
> *"You can do this, Johnny! I believe in you!"*
> *"Wow! He's never said anything like that to me before."*

You can be a person who fills people with doubt by discouraging them or help them succeed by offering ENCOURAGEMENT. Which would you want from others?

**_Power Memory Verse_** on the word **ENCOURAGEMENT**.

[16] *May our Lord Jesus Christ himself and God our Father, who loved us and by his grace gave us eternal encouragement and good hope,* [17] *encourage your hearts and strengthen you in every good deed and word. – 2 Thessalonians 2: 16-17*

# CHAPTER 9 - DOODLE PAGE
## Draw Your Favorite Memory from Chapter 9

# Chapter 10
# "LOVE"

Dictionary definition: "An intense feeling of deep affection."

Isn't it great feeling loved! Just knowing someone loves us can get us through the day with a smile. Johnny must have had a huge smile on his face when he saw how much LOVE his dad had for him. His dad was willing to risk his own safety for his son.

*"I instantly hugged my dad and didn't let go. I couldn't stop thanking him for saving me. He told me I had done most of the work myself but I knew that wasn't true. I knew inside he had saved me."*

Jesus says over and over again in the Bible that the greatest thing you can ever possess in life is love for one another. If there is someone in your life who you know loves you and would be there for you, maybe take some time to let them know you appreciate it. Especially a mom, dad, grandparent or someone close.

*Power Memory Verse* on the word **LOVE**.

*Jesus said:*
*"[13] Greater love has no one than this: to lay down one's life for one's friends. [14] You are my friends if you do what I command." – John 15: 13-14*

Show someone LOVE today!

# CHAPTER 10 - DOODLE PAGE
## Draw Your Favorite Memory from Chapter 10

# The Adventures of Johnny Lazarus
## BOOK SERIES

## Enjoy These Other JL Favorites

### BOOK 1: THE LEGEND OF FROG FINGER

**The Legend of Frog Finger** is a fast-pasted and fun adventure you won't want to miss! Follow Johnny, Henry and Richie as they attempt to take on a legendary 500 foot hill of doom known for chewing bike riders up and spitting them out! Johnny, and the reader, are guaranteed to learn a valuable lesson in this ride of a lifetime!

### BOOK 2: VINNIE'S STEAL ATTEMPT

**Vinnie's Steal Attempt** is a wild and almost unbelievable baseball adventure that Johnny himself wouldn't have believed had he not been there to see it. You might not believe it either, but you will laugh as you learn a valuable lesson about choosing the right direction for your life. A lesson Johnny's teammate Vinnie learns the hard way.

### BOOK 3: WAVE OF COURAGE

**Wave of Courage** is a non-stop, wild and crazy ocean adventure that challenges Johnny to be bolder than he has ever needed or wanted to be. With the encouragement of his good friend Tim, Johnny will be Challenged (dared) to do the unthinkable! Body-surf a mammoth, twenty-foot wave and live to tell about it!

# PROJECT

# Inspiring Kids to Share Jesus

### Creating Kid-Evangelists in One Easy Lesson!

Project316 is Keith Poletiek's outreach ministry for Children and Youth which challenge young believers to reach out and invite their unsaved family and friends to experience church: some for the first time ever!

## The Project316 Challenge!

ARE YOU
**READY
WILLING
& ABLE**

TO INVITE
**ONE
PERSON**
TO CHURCH

IN THE NEXT
**SIX
DAYS!**

# Over 6,500 Kids Have Said "YES!"

*"You'll be Amazed at the life-changing decisions your kids will make for themselves, their families and their unchurched friends - all in just thirty minutes time!"*
*- Keith Poletiek*

*"Growing Your Group From the Kid's-Side Out!*

**Call Today or Email with Questions or Availability**
As Always - We Work with ANY or NO BUDGET*
(*Must allow for Sales of Outreach Merchandise)
www.keithpoletiek.com   keith@threeonesix.org
## 951.201.2611

## Sunday Morning   Midweek   VBS   Camps/Events

*Project 316 is an amazing tool to help kids share their faith with their friends. It's encouraging, its helpful, its motivational, its fun and it works!*
*- Erin Gaxiola / Children's Pastor - Eastside Christian Church/Anaheim CA*

## About the Author
# Keith Poletiek

For the past 20+ years, Keith Poletiek has been traveling the nation sharing the Good News of Jesus using zany humor, memorable stories, life-lessons, and God's Word to connect with and inspire people of all ages.

Keith is the founder of 316 Studios and Project316, a national outreach ministry which challenges young believers to take the salvation message found in John 3:16 to their world.

Keith attended Pacific Christian College (now Hope International University) in Fullerton, CA as a Youth Ministry major and transitioned from there into youth ministry as the Junior High Pastor for Diamond Canyon Christian Church in Diamond Bar, CA and Eastside Christian Church in Anaheim, CA, before beginning his nationwide speaking ministry and book writing.

Along with being the author and illustrator of his popular Children's Christian Fiction book series, "The Adventures of Johnny Lazarus," Keith is also an Award Winning cartoonist and produces "Dude and Dude," an online, syndicated comic strip seen daily at GoComics.com (www.gocomics.com/dudedude).

Keith lives in Huntington Beach, CA, the town he grew up in, with his amazing wife of 31 years, Tina. All the Johnny Lazarus storylines are loosely based on events which Keith experienced during his childhood in this great city.

His has two grown children, Noah (29) and Myranda (25), and one granddaughter, Abella, who asked that her age not be made public.;)

Made in the USA
San Bernardino, CA
23 June 2018